the story

GRACE

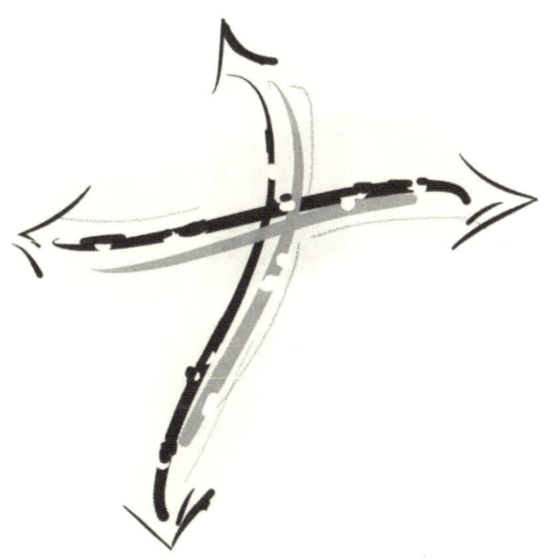

"When the story of God's Grace
intersects with the story of your life,
your life will never be the same."

brad robertson

The Story Of Grace
*When the story of God's grace intersects with the story of your life,
your life will never be the same!*

THE STORY OF GRACE
Copyright ©2018 by Brad Robertson

ISBN   9780692084946

Unless otherwise indicated, all Scripture quotations are taken from
the Holy Bible, *New International Version®*. NIV®. Copyright © 1973,
1978, 1984, 2011 by International Bible Society.

The names of people mentioned in this book have been changed.
However, the content of Brad's encounters with each of them is
true.

Printed In The United States of America

All rights reserved. No part of this publication may be reproduced,
stored in a retrieval system, or transformed in any form by any
means, electronic, mechanical, photocopy, recording, or any other,
without prior permission of the author. Except as provided by US
copyright law.

DEDICATION

I would like to dedicate this book to Bob George, author, teacher, and radio host. Along with his daily radio program, "People to People", Bob wrote *Classic Christianity, Growing In Grace, Faith That Pleases God*, and *Jesus Changes Everything*, among other books and Bible studies. It was through Bob's biblical teachings that my life was changed. Thank you, Bob, for your courage and persistence in teaching God's grace at a time when very few, if any, were teaching the good news of God's grace.

Because of your boldness in planting seeds of grace, we are seeing a harvest of changed lives all over the world. Many people are now sharing God's grace with others, which appropriately communicates the title of your radio program...*People to People*. In addition, grace-based churches are now being established all over the world!

At the time of the publication of *The Story Of Grace*, Bob's Health is in serious decline. He is no longer writing or teaching personally, but what he wrote and taught continues to change lives today.

On behalf of myself and many others, thank you, Bob, for clearly and courageously sharing the good news of God's grace. Our lives will never be the same, because, through your teachings, the story of God's grace intersected with the story of our lives.

ACKNOWLEDGMENTS

There is a person God brings into our lives who believes in us. This person continues to encourage us to pursue the dreams God puts into our hearts. For me, that person is my wife, Becky. She always believed I would write a book. She continually spoke words of encouragement to me and told me the book would be written in God's timing. That time has come. Without her words of encouragement, this book would still be a dream in my heart. Thank you, Becky, for your loving encouragement and support. Thank you for standing by me.

I would also like to acknowledge my three sons, Kyle, Philip, and Mark for the time they allowed me to invest in writing this book and the words of encouragement they, too, provided along the way. Like their mom, they believed in the dream God put into my heart and lovingly supported me in the process.

Thanks to Cathy Creel for her design of the cross used on the cover and throughout the book.

Thanks to Kyle Robertson and Sorg Printing for the cover design.

Thanks also to Josh Holland and Rick Sherrill, who invested many hours with my family and me in the editing process.

Thanks to the late J. Dwight Pentecost, former professor at Dallas Theological Seminary, for his dedicated efforts in writing his book and teaching his class *The Words and Works of Jesus Christ*. This book and class were invaluable to my understanding of God's coming kingdom.

Thanks to the late Lewis Sperry Chaffer for his book *Grace: An Exposition Of God's Marvelous Gift*. If only I could have taken one of his classes at Dallas Theological Seminary!

Thanks to Malcolm Smith. The Lord used the teachings of Malcolm Smith to reveal to me the depths of God's grace and love.

Finally, to my parents, Carroll and Barbara Robertson, who established a spiritual foundation for my life that God has used many wonderful people to build upon. Thank you, mom and dad, for the spiritual foundation you built in my life so that others would have a solid foundation on which to build.

CONTENTS

1

My Story Of Grace

When the story of God's grace intersects with the story of your life, your life will never be the same!

My Intersection With Grace

For me, it happened in 1991 while living in Boulder, Colorado, where I was on staff with *Campus Crusade for Christ*. I was about to fly home for a few days and was looking for a book to read during the flight. I asked a friend if she had one. She gave me a book called *Classic Christianity* by Bob George. Little did I know the story of God's grace was about to intersect with the story of my life.

During my flight, I could not put the book down. Page after page expounded on the grace of God given to us in Jesus. When I landed, my life was completely changed. While on an airplane from Denver to Mobile, the story of God's grace intersected with the story of my life. Since this encounter with grace, my life has never been the same.

Before reading *Classic Christianity*, I did not realize I was missing out on the heart of my relationship with God...grace. I could define grace as *God's unmerited favor*, which many people can do, but did not know the favor that was unmerited. I knew the acronym G.R.A.C.E., *God's Riches At Christ's Expense*, but did not know the riches of God's grace. I knew the song *Amazing Grace* but did not know why grace was so amazing. I knew we are saved by grace but did not understand the grace that saved us. I was practicing the spiritual disciplines such as attending church and Bible studies, participating in small groups, serving on a ministry team, reading my Bible, memorizing and meditating on Scripture, and having quiet times. I was leading Bible studies, speaking from time to time, and sharing Jesus with others. I was doing the "right things" spiritually but without any understanding of grace.

When I began reading *Classic Christianity*, I realized, that even though I was familiar with the word grace, I really didn't understand its full meaning. By not understanding the complete meaning of grace, I totally missed the heart of Christianity. It wasn't until I read *Classic Christianity* that I discovered what I missed out on for years, the story of God's grace.

I must admit, even though my heart leapt for joy when I read the biblical truth of grace contained in *Classic Christianity*, my mind found it difficult to accept. Accepting the total message of grace as biblical truth was difficult because I was never taught grace in its fullness. The truth I was reading about in *Classic Christianity* was contrary to much of what I had learned as a Christian and what I was teaching. So, I set off on a journey into the Bible to see what was true.

My Journey Into Grace

For my entire life as a Christian, I assumed much of what I heard from a Bible teacher, preacher, author, or mentor was true. It never occurred to me to compare their words with God's word. But after reading *Classic Christianity*, I decided to compare the words I heard from people, including the words of Bob George in *Classic Christianity*, with the word of God. I could no longer accept the words of others as truth. I made this mistake for far too long. It was time for me to compare their words with God's word.

As I began making this comparison, it became obvious I was never fully taught the truth of God's grace. The words of others were not aligning with the word of God. It was at this point I had a decision to make, a crisis of faith I guess you could say. Was I going to place my faith in the word of God or in the words of others? I made the decision to place my faith in the word of God, the Bible.

Making this decision wasn't easy. This was because my beliefs were based on what I was previously taught. To believe differently just didn't feel right. Yet I knew I could not put the words of people above the word of God. Even though the words of others were deeply embedded in my mind, I realized I must forgo my feelings and place my faith in God's word. I understood my feelings were not the measurement of truth, God's word is. So, I denied my feelings and placed my faith in God's word instead of the words of others.

This biblical journey, which started in my life after reading *Classic Christianity,* continues today. On this journey, I have learned to study the Bible in context. By this, I mean the covenant I am reading, old or new, the context of the book, chapter, and verse I am reading, and how the small part of the Bible I am reading fits into its larger story.

I have learned the greatest commentary on the Bible is the Bible itself. Even though commentaries are helpful in studying the Bible, they are not the word of God. Commentaries are simply people's words about God's word. I remember what Bob George said during one of his radio programs, *"The Bible sure will shed a lot of light on those commentaries."* Often, we use commentaries to shed light on God's word, and sometimes they do, but not always. When studying the Bible, we should first see if God's word sheds light on itself before reading commentaries. Then, when it does, we should always place our faith in God's word rather than the words of others.

I also learned notes provided in study Bibles may or may not be accurate. They definitely are not all in agreement. Study Bibles simply provide a person's or a group of people's interpretations of the Bible. I am not saying study Bible notes aren't helpful, but we can't make the notes infallible.

Once in a class I was teaching, a person commented that the notes in his study Bible were different than what I was teaching. He could not accept I would have a different understanding than that of his study Bible notes. To him, his study Bible notes were equal with the Bible itself, and there was no convincing him otherwise. This is a great example of how others' words can become more important than God's word. When this happens, we become more consumed with what is traditional than what is biblical.

Traditional Versus Biblical

It is easy for us to become deeply rooted in what is traditional, the words of others, rather than what is biblical, the word of God. Speaking to this common mistake of valuing the words of others above the word of God, Jesus said, *"You have let go of the commands of God and are holding on to the traditions of men...You have a fine way of setting aside the commands of God in order to observe your own traditions!...Thus, You nullify the word of God for the sake of your tradition that you have handed down. And you do many things like that"* (Mark 7:8-13).

Jesus spoke these words to the Pharisees and teachers of the Law of Moses when they asked him why his disciples did not live according to the traditions of their elders. The Pharisees and teachers of the law, the religious leaders during Jesus' time, were deeply rooted in their traditional teachings. Jesus, nor his disciples, followed their teachings. This made them very upset with Jesus. In their anger, they would confront Jesus about his departure from their traditional teachings, which they did in this situation.

What we learn in this exchange between Jesus, the Pharisees, and the teachers of the law is what is traditional is often accepted as biblical, when, it is not biblical at all. Yet what is traditional continues to be passed down and accepted as biblical. When what is traditional is challenged, as Jesus challenged the traditional teachings of the religious leaders, the biblical teaching is rejected as heresy. Those who reject the biblical teaching become angry at those rejecting the traditional teaching in the same way the religious leaders became angry toward Jesus. The legalistic, performance-based teachings of religious teachers, passed down from one generation to the next, have become so widespread and accepted that the teaching of grace is considered a strange teaching and, therefore, is automatically rejected by many in churches, especially by church leaders.

I think this emphasis on what is traditional over what is biblical is why grace remains a strange, unfamiliar teaching to believers today. Because the teaching of grace is strange to many believers, some reply by saying, *"Why has no one ever taught me this before? It is right here in the Bible. It's so clear. It's so obvious. Why is grace not taught in churches?"* These are people who have been active in their churches for years but have never been taught the good news of God's grace. When they are finally taught the transforming truths of grace, they are amazed no one ever taught them about grace.

One person who had been in church for years attended a class I was teaching on grace. After the class, he told me, *"I have sung Amazing Grace a thousand times, but I never knew what grace was until I took your classes."*

Another person, a lady in her late sixties, had a similar experience when taking my class on grace. After the class, she asked me, *"Why has no one ever taught me about grace?"* This lady was raised in a church and was a Sunday School teacher. I started thinking about how many sermons she heard over the course of her life. Since she consistently attended church on Sunday mornings and nights, as well as Wednesday nights, that would have her hearing well over six thousand sermons in her lifetime. This does not include the Sunday School classes she attended, as well as the conferences or retreats she may have attended.

Sadly, I have discovered her experience is a common experience among many, if not most, people in churches. Like this lady, many people who have been in churches for most of their lives are unfamiliar with the teaching of grace. This is because traditional teachings have replaced the biblical truth of grace.

In the Bible, Paul was one of the Pharisees extremely zealous for the traditional teachings of his forefathers, but it was the truth of grace that set him free.

> *"I was advancing in Judaism beyond many Jews of my own age and was extremely zealous for the traditions of my fathers. But when God, who set me apart from birth and called me by his grace, was pleased to reveal his Son in me so that I might preach him among the Gentiles..."*
>
> Galatians 1:14

Because of the revelation of grace, Paul broke free from the traditions to which he was once so committed. In breaking free, he became consumed with sharing God's grace with others. I can relate to that!

The Bible Is Logical

The Bible is the story of God's grace. It is a very logical story. Each book of the Bible and each verse of the book fits in logically with all the other books and verses of the Bible to tell its story. Trying to understand the books of the Bible and verses without understanding how they fit into the larger story leads to confusion, poor interpretation, and misapplication.

Through this book, I hope to educate people about the larger story of grace the Bible tells and how the books and verses of the Bible fit into the story. By doing this, it is my desire to help people understand the Bible as never before.

As you read through the following chapters of this book, remember, these are only my words about God's word. I would suggest you compare everything I say in this book with the word of God. I do not presume to know all truths. However, I have done my best to study the Bible in context and present to you my understanding of God's word.

Making Grace Crystal Clear

In 1922, Lewis Sperry Chafer, a highly respected Bible teacher in his time and founder of Dallas Theological Seminary, stated in his book, *Grace: An Exposition of God's Marvelous Gift*, the following:

> *The exact and discriminate meaning of the word*
> *grace should be crystal clear to every child of God.*
> *With such insight only can he feed his own soul on the*
> *inexhaustible riches which unfolds, and with such*
> *understanding only can he be enabled clearly to pass*
> *on to others its marvelous, transforming theme* (page
> 19).

Making the message of grace crystal clear to every child of God has become my passion. Since the day the story of God's grace intersected with the story of my life, it has been my passion to share the story of his grace with as many people as possible in as many ways as possible. This book is just one of the ways I can share the story of his grace. My prayer is, as you read this book, the story of God's grace intersects with the story of your life, and your life will never be the same!

2

The Story Of Grace Begins

The story of grace begins in the heart of God. To fully appreciate this story, we must first go back to before time began and examine why God created anything or anyone at all.

The Purpose Of Time

The Bible says that before time began, God gave us grace in Christ.

> *This grace was given us in Christ before the beginning*
> *of time...*
>
> 2 Timothy 1:9

Think about what this means...if grace was given to us in Christ before the beginning of time, the purpose of time must be for the unveiling of grace by God to those for whom it was given. Steven Curtis Chapman captures this purpose for time in his song *The Glorious Unfolding*:

> *God's plan from the start for this world and your*
> *heart has been to show his glory and his grace.*
> *Forever revealing the depth and the beauty of his*
> *unfailing love.*

What Is Grace?

The purpose of time is for the story of God's grace to intersect with the story of your life. Once this happens, your life will never be the same. Since the purpose of time is God's revelation of grace to the human race, then what is grace?

> *Grace is God's unconditional love, unearned blessings, unmerited kindness, and unlimited forgiveness freely given to us through Jesus Christ for the purpose of reconciling us to himself in a love relationship and restoring the earth to its original condition for our enjoyment.*

About grace, Lewis Sperry Chafer says:

> *When used in the Bible to set forth the grace of God in the salvation of sinners, the word grace not only discloses the boundless goodness and kindness of God toward humanity, but reaches far beyond and indicates the supreme motive which actuated God in the creation, preservation and consummation of the universe. What greater fact could be expressed by one word?* (Grace: An Exposition of God's Marvelous Gift, page 19)

He also says:

> *No one word in all the Bible more fully describes God's plans and purposes than "grace".* (Back cover)

So, let's go back...way back...to before time began and take a closer look into the heart of God, where grace began.

Created By God

Before time began, God existed. His nature was love. It was this love that moved him to create mankind. The Bible says God is love (1 John 4:16), and that we were created in his image (Genesis 1:27). This means we were created to be loved by God and to love God. We were created by God to be in a love relationship with him. This is the purpose for our existence.

Not only did God create us to be in a love relationship with him, but he also created all things for our enjoyment. God created earth and everything in it for the enjoyment of those he loved. Once God completed his creation, the Bible says, *"He saw all that he had made, and it was very good"* (Genesis 1:31). From this point forward, the role of mankind was to enjoy all the good God had created.

Walking Away From God

Following his creation of mankind, God commanded Adam not to eat from the tree of the knowledge of good and evil. God told Adam that if he ate from the tree, he would die. The reason God gave Adam a choice to eat or not to eat from the tree was because a relationship is not a relationship unless someone has the choice to be or not be in the relationship. Therefore, God gave Adam a choice whether he wanted to be in a relationship with him.

Had God not given Adam a choice, Adam would have only been a robot programmed to love God. Yet Adam was not a robot. He was created in God's image with the ability to choose, and the tree of the knowledge of good and evil presented him this opportunity. Adam chose to eat from the tree. In eating from the tree, he walked away from his love relationship with God. Adam's act of walking away from God is called sin. And with this act of sin, sin and death entered the world and spread to the entire human race (Romans 5:12).

Sin And Death Spread To The Human Race

Because sin and death spread to the entire human race, everyone is born spiritually dead, or separated from a love relationship with God. Sin replaced the love of God in our hearts. Sin produces evil, jealousy, coveting, lying, hatred, anger, impatience, unkindness, rudeness, fear, immorality, unfaithfulness, harshness, pride, and arrogance, along with many other sinful attitudes, actions, and desires. Through sin, the human heart became desperately wicked and deceitful (Jeremiah 17:9). Nothing good comes from the heart. According to Jesus, out of the heart comes evil thoughts, desires, and deeds (Matthew 15:9). The effects of sin on the human heart are at the core of all family, social, national, and world problems.

Sin Affected All Of Creation

In addition to mankind being separated from God because of sin, affecting the heart of mankind and the world we live in, all of God's creation was affected by sin. Because of sin, creation itself is not the same. What God originally called good, when looking at all he created, was no longer good. Things changed. The atmosphere was affected. The climate was affected. The only thing not affected by sin was God's love for mankind. Because he loved us so much, he longed to bring salvation to us by reconciling us to himself in a love relationship and restoring the earth to its original condition.

God Still Loves Us

Despite our sin, God still loved us and desired to be in a relationship with us. He still wanted us to enjoy the earth he created. In fact, our sin was the perfect way for God to unveil his grace to us.

God had a plan before time began. It was a plan of grace by which he would pour out his unconditional love, unearned blessings, unmerited kindness, and unlimited forgiveness on us. The unveiling of his plan is the story of grace.

The story of grace is seen in Romans 5:15:

> *For if the many* [the human race] *died by the trespass of the one man* [Adam]*, how much more did God's grace and the gift that came by the grace of the one man, Jesus Christ, overflow to the many!*

The sin of Adam did not take God by surprise. God is all-knowing. In his omniscience, he knew mankind would walk away from a love relationship with him. Because of this knowledge, he provided grace for us in Christ before time began so we could be reconciled to him and so all things could be restored to their original condition.

The working out of God's grace plan began immediately after the sin of Adam. God replaced the fig leaves, which Adam and his wife covered themselves, with animal skins. For Adam and Eve to be clothed with animal skins, an innocent animal had to die. So rather than Adam and Eve dying for their sins, the animal was substituted in their place. This was a picture of grace carried on throughout future generations in the Bible until Jesus, through grace, was substituted in our place, and through his blood made the full and final payment for all sins, for all people, for all time.

God revealed more of his story of grace to Adam and Eve when he said a woman would give birth to a male child who would crush Satan's head (Genesis 3:15). God was making a promise that One would come to bring grace to the world. Through this Promised One, God would reconcile the people of the world to himself in a love relationship and restore the earth to its original condition. The Promised One would bring the story of grace to earth.

From where would this Promised One come? What woman would give birth to him? Who would he be? And what would he do?

3

The Story Of The Promised One

In Genesis 12:1-3, God called a man from the human race through whom he continued to unveil the story of grace. This man would be the father of a great nation, and this nation would be a blessing to all people. From this nation, the Promised One, who would bring grace to the people of the world, would be born. He would reconcile humanity to God in a love relationship and restore everything to its original condition for our enjoyment. He would be named Jesus.

God Calls One Man

The man whom God called to be a father of this great nation was named Abram, later renamed Abraham. The nation was named Israel. God promised he would bless all people and nations on earth through Israel.

> *The Lord said to Abram, "Leave your country, your people, and your father's household and go to the land I will show you. I will make you into a great nation and I will bless you; I will make your name great and you will be a blessing. I will bless those who bless you and whoever curses you I will curse; and all peoples* [nations] *on earth will be blessed through you."*
>
> Genesis 12:1-3

We see in these verses God's heart of love for people all over the world. People in every nation, every city, every community, every neighborhood, every village, and every place are loved by God. Because of his love, he desired and promised to bless all those living on earth. This blessing was the promise of grace expressed in his kindness to us through Jesus. Through grace, he would reconcile us to himself in a love relationship and restore the earth to its original condition.

A Name Change

This promise of grace is reflected when God changed Abram's name to Abraham and Sarai's, Abram's wife, name to Sarah.

> *"No longer will you be called Abram; your name will*
> *be called Abraham… As for Sarai your wife, you are*
> *no longer to call her Sarai; her name will be Sarah."*
>
> Genesis 17:5, 15

The name change reflected by the addition of the letter "h" to Abram's and Sarai's names represented God breathing life into the human race through grace. The letter "h" in the Hebrew language means *breath of life*. Each letter of the Hebrew alphabet also has a corresponding number. The corresponding number for "h" is five. Five is the number for grace in the Hebrew language. By adding the "h" to the names of Abram and Sarai, which by the way is in the fifth spot of their names, God was communicating to us he was going to bless the human race through grace by breathing life back into us, the very life sin took out of us.

In the creation story, God breathed the breath of life into mankind:

The Lord God formed the man from the dust of the
ground and breathed into his nostrils the breath of
life, and man became a living being.

Genesis 2:7

However, after mankind walked away from a love relationship with God, sin and death entered the human race, severing our love relationship with God. A love relationship with God is what life is all about. So, when mankind walked away from God, we walked away from our very source of life. This would be like a fish choosing to live separated from the water. If a fish chooses to live apart from the water, it severs itself from its very source of life because everything the fish needs for life is in the water. Life for a fish is the water.

What water is to a fish, God is to us. Separating a fish from the water is like separating mankind from God. Both have been separated from their very source of life. Apart from the water, a fish dies. Apart from God, mankind dies. The greatest need of a fish is to be reconciled to the water. The greatest need of mankind is to be reconciled to God in a love relationship. Only then will we have life. And how would we be reconciled to God? Through grace!

Grace Brings Life!

Life for mankind would be restored through grace! Only through grace could we ever experience life again.

For if, by the trespass of the one man, death reigned
through the one man, how much more will those who
receive God's abundant provision of grace and the
gift of righteousness reign in life through the one

*man, Jesus Christ. Consequently, just as the result of
one trespass was condemnation for all men, so also
the one act of righteousness was justification that
brought life for all men…just as sin reigned in death,
so also grace might reign through righteousness to
bring eternal life through Jesus Christ our Lord.*

Romans 5:17-21

Through Jesus, God poured grace into the human race, restoring us to life. This is why we see so many references in the Bible combining Jesus and life together. In the book of John, the word *life* is spoken by Jesus over forty times, referring to himself bringing life to the people of the world. The following verses are examples of this:

I am the bread of life… John 6:35

I am the resurrection and the life… John 11:5

I am the way and the truth and the life… John 14:6

Through grace, God would breathe life into us by reconciling us to himself in a love relationship. This grace, promised by God to Abraham, would come to us through the nation of Israel, specifically through Jesus. This is seen in the following verses:

*Consider Abraham: "He believed God, and it was
credited to him as righteousness." Understand, then,
that those who believe are children of Abraham. The
Scripture foresaw that God would justify the Gentiles
by faith, and announced the gospel [grace] in*

advance to Abraham: "All nations will be blessed through you." So those who have faith are blessed along with Abraham, the man of faith...

Galatians 3:6-9

...the blessing given to Abraham might come to the Gentiles [everyone all over the world] through Christ Jesus...God in his grace gave it to Abraham through a promise...

Galatians 3:14, 18

The Scripture declares that the whole world is a prisoner of sin, so that what was promised, being given through faith in Jesus Christ, might be given to those who believe...Before this faith came, we were held prisoners by the law...the law was put in charge to lead us to Christ that we might be justified by faith...If you belong to Christ, then you are Abraham's seed, and heirs according to the promise...

Galatians 3:22-24, 29

But when the time had fully come, God sent his Son, born of a woman, born under law, to redeem those under law, that we might receive the full rights as sons. Because you are sons, God sent the Spirit of his Son into our hearts, the Spirit who calls out, "Abba, Father."

Galatians 4:4-6

> *Therefore, the promise comes by faith, so that it may be by grace and guaranteed to all Abraham's offspring...*
>
> Romans 4:16

> *Therefore, since we have been justified through faith, we have peace with God through our Lord Jesus Christ, through whom we have gained access by faith into this grace in which we now stand.*
>
> Romans 5:1-2

So, what is the promise of grace God made to Abraham? Based upon the previous verses, I summarize God's promise of grace to bless the people of the world as follows:

> *God's desire is to have a love relationship with everyone. He accomplished this through grace, which is his unconditional love, unearned blessings, unmerited kindness, and unlimited forgiveness freely given to us through Jesus. God made a promise to Abraham to bless, or grace, the people of the world through the nation of Israel, specifically through Jesus who was a descendant of Abraham. Through God's blessing of grace, expressed in his love, kindness, and forgiveness to us in Jesus, the penalty of sin for all people was paid. This promise of grace includes being reconciled to God, declared not guilty by God (justified), made righteous before God (cleansed from all sin), forgiven by God, and removed from the law. We enter God's grace by faith. Through faith in Jesus,*

we can begin a love relationship with God. When we place our faith in Jesus, God sends the Spirit of his Son into our hearts, enabling us to call him "Abba, Father" and allowing us to enjoy a genuine relationship with him.

In fulfilling his promise of grace, God called Abraham to leave where he was and go to a land God would show him. This land was Canaan. So, Abraham went to the land of Canaan, also known as the Promised Land. This land, the very place from where God's story of grace would come, became the homeland of the nation of Israel and the birthplace of Jesus.

The Promised King And Kingdom

The Promised King

The Old Testament records the history of the nation of Israel, foretelling of a child from Israel who will bring grace to the world. He will be a king. He will be born in Bethlehem (Micah 5:2) from the family line of David, Israel's second king (Isaiah 9:6-7; Jeremiah 33:15-16).

As the King of Israel, he will establish God's eternal kingdom of love, peace, joy, gladness, healing, and righteousness on earth. Every corner of the world and every person in the world will be touched by his love! The following verses reveal this coming King and kingdom he will establish: Isaiah 9:6-7; 2:2-4; 11:1-10; 35:5-6; 40:5; Daniel 2:44; 7:27; Zechariah 9:9-19; 12:9; Psalm 22:27-28; 67:1-7; 117:1-2; 145:13.

This King will usher in God's blessing of grace to the world. This blessing includes peace among the animal kingdom and peace among the nations of the world. There will be no more war. Peace will flow from one end of the earth to the other. There will be social, emotional, mental, financial, and relational peace. Peace will be known across the earth and experienced and enjoyed by everyone. It will be a place where everything is right and everyone is loved!

Eventually, there will be a new heaven and a new earth.

Behold I will create new heavens and a new earth.
Isaiah 65:17

But in keeping with his promise, we are looking
forward to a new heaven and a new earth, the home
of righteousness.
2 Peter 3:13

What Is This Kingdom Called?

This coming eternal kingdom of love, peace, joy, gladness, healing, and righteousness is called the kingdom of God or the kingdom of heaven. It is referred to by Jesus in what is commonly called the Lord's Prayer when he says, "*Your kingdom come your will be done on earth as it is in heaven*" (Matthew 6:10). It will have its beginning on the earth we currently live on, but it will find its ultimate fulfillment on the new earth.

The King Will Be A Savior

This coming King will also be the Savior of the world. He will provide the opportunity for everyone to be a part of God's kingdom by dying for our sins. He is described as the Servant who gives his life for the sins of all mankind and then rises from the dead (Isaiah 53; Psalm 16:10; 22).

Can you imagine it? Russia, China, North Korea, India, Pakistan, Iran, Iraq, Germany, Spain, Australia, Mexico, Brazil, Libya, Kenya, Uganda, Canada, the United States and every other nation on earth under the rule and reign of this Savior-King, with his love, peace, joy, gladness, healing, and righteousness filling every person in every home in every nation.

What Is The King Called?

This Promised One, coming into the world through Israel, is called in the Old Testament, *Messiah,* and in the New Testament, *Christ*. The Messiah, or Christ, is the one who ushers in God's grace to save mankind from their sins as Savior and bring eternal love, peace, joy, gladness, healing, and righteousness into the world as King. The Messiah or Christ is the one sent by God to bring grace to the people of the world, reconciling mankind to God in a love relationship and restoring the earth to its original condition.

Concerning the coming of the Christ, the prophets in the Old Testament and the angels desired to look further into the grace he would bring to the human race. 1 Peter 1:10-12 says:

> *Concerning this salvation, the prophets, who spoke to you, of the grace that was to come to you, searched intently and with the greatest of care, trying to find out the time and circumstances to which the Spirit of Christ in them was pointing when he predicted the sufferings of Christ and the glories that would follow...Even angels long to look into these things.*

The Genealogy of Jesus

In Matthew chapter one, the first seventeen verses record the genealogy of Jesus. Why? Because the Old Testament foretells the Messiah or Christ, who was to come to establish the kingdom of God on earth, would be born in the family line of David and Abraham. Therefore, Matthew 1:1-17 records the genealogy of Jesus to prove to the reader that Jesus is the Messiah, or Christ, foretold in the Old Testament. The remainder of the book of Matthew is written to prove Jesus really is the Christ.

The Forerunner Of The Christ

Before the coming of the Christ, the Old Testament spoke of a forerunner who would come, announcing the arrival of the Christ to Israel and preparing the nation for his arrival and his salvation (Isaiah 40:3-5; Malachi 4:5-6). The forerunner of the Christ was called John the Baptist whose father was Zechariah.

Zechariah was a priest who served in the temple of Israel in Jerusalem. When Zechariah was in the Holy Place of the temple, the angel Gabriel appeared to him, telling him his wife, Elizabeth, would give birth to a son and his name was to be John. Their son would be the forerunner of the Christ (Luke 1:5-25).

Six months after Elizabeth became pregnant, God sent the angel Gabriel to Nazareth. He appeared to Mary, telling her she would give birth to the Christ, and he would establish God's kingdom on earth. She was instructed by Gabriel to give the child the name Jesus (Luke 1:26-38).

The Purpose Of The Names

In both angelic appearances, Gabriel provided the names Elizabeth and Mary were to name their children, John and Jesus. But what is so significant about these names? Why would it matter what they were named? Why would God have Gabriel instruct the parents to name the children John and Jesus? Certainly God, in giving Gabriel the exact names for these two children, had a purpose behind these names. But what was his purpose?

Jewish names always had a meaning. Once we see the meaning of the names John and Jesus, as well as Zechariah, Elizabeth, and Mary, God's purpose for these names will be clearly seen. Let's look at the meaning of these names.

John's father's name was Zechariah. The name Zechariah means *God Remembers*.

John's mother's name was Elizabeth. The name Elizabeth means *God's Promise*.

John means *Grace*.

Jesus means *Savior*.

Mary means *Loved One*.

Now, let's put all these names together and then the purpose of the names John and Jesus will be crystal clear.

God remembers his promise of grace to save those he loves.

Amazing! God is so loving toward those who walked away from him, which is all of us, that even the names of those involved in the story of grace reflect his continued love for all mankind and his desire to be in a love relationship with us. The meaning of these names communicates God's story of grace, the grace which he gave us in Christ before the beginning of time.

This promise of grace, to reconcile us to himself in a love relationship and to restore the earth to its original condition, was given to us in Christ by God before the beginning of time, revealed to us over the course of time, and appeared to us in God's perfect time. This perfect time was the appearance of grace through a baby born in a manger.

> *But when the time had fully come, God sent his Son,*
> *born of a woman...*
>
> Galatians 4:4

> *For the grace of God that brings salvation has*
> *appeared to all men...*
>
> Titus 2:11

The Birth Of The Christ, The Birth Of Grace!

Christmas is the birth of grace! It is the birth of the Christ, Jesus, who was born as Savior-King for the very purpose of unfolding God's story of grace to the world. The Christ, the Promised Savior-King, was born exactly where the Old Testament said he would be born, Bethlehem, to be exactly who the Old Testament said he would be, Savior-King, and to do exactly what the Old Testament said he would do, bring peace on earth.

This good news was announced by an angel to the shepherds.

> *"Do not be afraid. I bring you good news of great joy*
> *that will be for all the people. Today in the town of*

> *David* [Bethlehem] *a Savior has been born to you; he*
> *is Christ the Lord* [King]*."*
>
> Luke 2:10-11

The angel who made this announcement to the shepherds was then joined by a heavenly host, and together they began praising God, saying together:

> *"Glory to God in the highest, and on earth peace to*
> *men on whom his favor [**grace**] rests."*
>
> Luke 2:13-14

This Savior-King, the Promised One, was born! The angel announced this good news of great joy that was for all people. The Christ, who was to come to bless the people of the world through grace, had been born!

The Bible speaks about the arrival of God's grace in Jesus.

> *In the beginning was the Word and the Word was*
> *with God and the Word was God...The Word became*
> *flesh [Jesus] and made his dwelling among us...From*
> *the fullness of his **grace** we have all received one*
> *blessing after another.*
>
> John 1:1-2, 14, 16

God Reconciled The World To Himself Through Christ

The Bible also speaks about God's grace given through Jesus to reconcile us to himself in a love relationship.

> *All this is from God, who reconciled us to himself*
> *through Christ and gave us the ministry of*

reconciliation: that God was reconciling the world to himself in Christ, not counting men's sins against them. And he has committed to us the message of reconciliation. We are therefore Christ's ambassadors, as though God was making his appeal through us. We implore you on Christ's behalf: Be reconciled to God. God made him who had no sin to be sin for us, so that in him we might become the righteousness of God. As God's fellow workers we urge you not to receive [hear about] *God's grace in vain...I tell you, now is the time of God's favor* [grace]*, now is the day of salvation.*

2 Corinthians 5:18-6:2

The Rejection, Resurrection, And Return Of The Christ

The Christ, born into the world to bring God's grace, was rejected by the world he came to save. The people of Israel declared Jesus was not their king, demanding he be crucified (John 19). The Gentiles nailed him to the cross. The whole world rallied against him!

Yet he rose from the dead, ascended into heaven, and will one day return as King to usher in God's eternal kingdom of love, peace, joy, gladness, healing, and righteousness on earth, eventually establishing his kingdom on the new earth (Revelations 11:15; 21:1-5).

The New Earth

The new earth is the restoration of the earth to its original condition for humanity's enjoyment. It is the home of God's eternal kingdom of love, peace, joy, gladness, healing, and righteousness. It is what people all over the world long for deep within their hearts. It will be a place of total healing and happiness. It will be a place of total peace and purity. There will be no more pain, sorrow, mourning, fear, or death. There will be no more disease or deformity. There will be no war. People will live together in complete harmony and unity. All things will be new!

We will enjoy, explore, develop, and manage the new earth. We will build, work, and play on the new earth. We will enjoy athletics, music, friendships, hunting, fishing, painting, movies, theater, etc... We will develop the new earth through architecture, engineering, and construction. All the things we enjoy on the earth now, we will enjoy on the new earth, except the new earth will not be affected by sin or Satan.

We will have new bodies to live on the new earth, bodies which will never grow old. We will enjoy the new earth at a greater level of enjoyment than ever before, because it is the home of righteousness where everything is right. The limitless possibilities of what the new earth offers are beyond imagination!

And what makes all this possible? Grace! Even though we walked away from God, he did not walk away from us. In grace, Jesus came to us. He came to us in a manger. He died for our sins on a cross. He rose from the dead to give us life, and he will return to reign as King. It will be God's good pleasure to bring his story of grace to fulfillment through the return of Jesus, when all things in heaven and earth will be brought together under his reign (Ephesians 1:9-10).

The time is coming when God's story of grace will be fulfilled, and we will forever enjoy the eternal inheritance of grace in his kingdom. For all eternity, people all over the world will celebrate the marvelous grace of God...his unconditional love, unearned blessings, unmerited kindness, and unlimited forgiveness lavished upon us in Christ Jesus. In the coming age, when we are living in God's eternal kingdom, we will be the objects of his grace for all eternity!

> *...in the coming ages he might show the incomparable riches of his **grace**, expressed in his kindness to us in Christ Jesus.*
>
> Ephesians 2:7

Until then, God's grace will be with all his people (Revelation 22:21).

Let's now take a closer look at the story of the King and his kingdom.

4

The Story Of The King And His Kingdom

In the previous chapters, we learned God sent a male child into the world through the nation of Israel as Savior-King to bring grace to the world. This Savior-King is called Messiah, or Christ. He came to reconcile the people of the world to God in a love relationship by dying for our sins and establishing God's eternal kingdom.

In this chapter, we will continue to examine the story of grace by taking a closer look at Jesus, the kingdom he will rule over, and the responses of the people of Israel and the world to his coming.

Longing For The Kingdom Of God

In the New Testament, this coming eternal kingdom is called both the kingdom of God and the kingdom of heaven. They are synonymous. In the Old Testament, God promised this kingdom would first come to the nation of Israel, then to the world. We have already seen many verses in the Old Testament revealing this coming kingdom.

For many years, the people of Israel deeply desired and expected the coming of the Christ who would establish the kingdom of heaven upon earth. They had been conquered by other nations and were in tremendous oppression. Consequently, they longed for the promises of the King and kingdom to be fulfilled.

One who longed for the coming of the Christ was Zechariah. As discussed earlier in chapter three, the angel Gabriel appeared to him inside the temple, informing him that his wife, Elizabeth, would give birth to a son who was to be named John. John would be the forerunner of the Christ, Israel's and the world's coming Savior-King.

The Kingdom Of Heaven Is Near

At about the age of 30, John began his ministry of preparing the people of Israel for the coming of the Christ and the establishment of his kingdom when all mankind would see God's salvation (Luke 3:6). His message to the people of Israel was *"Repent, for the kingdom of heaven is near"* (Matthew 3:1-2). John announced the good news to the people of Israel that the long-awaited King and kingdom was soon to arrive, and the people needed to repent by recognizing God's kindness, admitting their sins, and accepting God's forgiveness in preparation of the King and the establishment of the kingdom.

The phrase used to describe the announcement of the kingdom was called *"the gospel of the kingdom"* or *"the good news of the kingdom"* (Mark 1:14-15). The word *gospel* means *good news*. The people needed to hear the good news that God's eternal kingdom of love, peace, joy, gladness, healing, and righteousness was ready to be established on earth. It is the same good news we long to hear as well. In a world where terror, tragedy, death, fear, doubt, confusion, injustice, and problems dominate the headlines of our newspapers and lead stories on our television news channels and internet news sites, we, too, could use some good news about God's coming kingdom.

After John's ministry of preparing the people of Israel for the arrival of the King and his kingdom, Jesus, the Christ, took center stage. Jesus and his disciples went throughout the cities, towns, and villages of Israel announcing the good news that the kingdom of God was at hand (Matthew 4:17, 23, 9:35, 10:7; Luke 4:43, 8:1, 9:2, 11; 10:9).

In the Bible, the message of the kingdom of God was the heart of Jesus' teaching in the books of Matthew, Mark, Luke, and John. Many of his parables centered on the coming kingdom to earth. He even taught his disciples to pray for the kingdom of God to come to earth (Matthew 6:10).

The phrase *gospel of the kingdom* is important to know because in later chapters of this book we will learn about the connection of the gospel of the kingdom to the gospel of grace. By understanding the gospel of the kingdom and the gospel of grace, we will have a greater understanding of the story of grace. But for now, we are focusing on the good news of the kingdom.

Could Jesus Be The Christ?

As the good news of the kingdom spread throughout the cities, towns, and villages of Israel, the people began to debate among themselves whether Jesus was truly the Christ, the Promised King sent by God to establish his eternal kingdom on earth (John 4:29; 7:25-44; Mark 8:27-29). The pages of Matthew, Mark, Luke, and John reveal the debates happening among the people. In their minds and conversations was one dominant question, *"Could Jesus really be the long-awaited Christ, the Promised Savior-King, who is to establish God's eternal kingdom on earth?"*

According to the Old Testament, when Christ came, he would heal the deaf, lame, and blind (Isaiah 35:4-6; Malachi 4:2). Health and wholeness would be the experience of all in God's kingdom (Psalm 103:3).

John, right before his death, sent his own disciples to ask Jesus if he really was the Christ. To confirm he was indeed the Christ, Jesus replied, *"Go back and report to John what you hear and see: The blind receive sight, the lame walk, those who have leprosy are cured, the deaf hear, the dead are raised, and the good news is preached to the poor"* (Matthew 11:2-5).

The Old Testament said Christ would be full of grace in how he spoke to and treated people (Psalm 45:2; Isaiah 61:1-3). He would proclaim the good news of grace to those in spiritual poverty, meaning those broken in their sin (Isaiah 61:1-3). Forgiveness and freedom would be the experience of all those who received his grace (Luke 4:14-19). And when he came, he was full of grace, just as the Old Testament said he would be (John 1:14, 16; Luke 4:16-22).

For three years, this question of Jesus being the Christ continued to be heatedly discussed by the people of Israel. But, in the end, only a few accepted him as King. Sadly, most rejected him. Eventually, the people of Israel concluded he was not their King and called for his crucifixion (John 19:14-16). So together with the Roman government, the people of Israel had their King crucified (Acts 2:23). Yet this King rose from the dead (Luke 24:6), just as he and the Old Testament Scriptures said he would (Acts 2:27). This act of rejection of the Christ by Israel and the world, along with the resurrection, was all a part of God's sovereign plan to bring salvation to the world (Acts 2:22-32; 3:17-18).

Jesus Teaches On The Kingdom

After his resurrection, Jesus appeared to his followers for over a period of forty days, teaching them about the kingdom of God. As he taught on the kingdom of God, they asked him an obvious question, *"Lord, are you at this time going to restore the kingdom to Israel?"* By this, they were asking Jesus if he was about to establish God's kingdom of love, peace, joy, gladness, healing, and righteousness on earth. Jesus' response was that they were not to be concerned with the times and dates of the establishment of the kingdom of God, but they were to await the coming of the Holy Spirit who would empower them to be his witnesses in Jerusalem, Judea, Samaria, and to the ends of the earth (Acts 1:1-8).

Following Jesus' ascension into heaven, his followers were gathered together in one house when the Holy Spirit came upon them. The time of this gathering was during the time of Pentecost. Pentecost was a Jewish celebration, attracting Jewish people from all over the known world to Jerusalem.

It was at this time, when thousands of Jewish people gathered in Jerusalem for the Pentecost celebration, the Holy Spirit descended upon the followers of Jesus, enabling them to speak in the tongues, or the languages, of all those who were gathered in Jerusalem for this celebration. Amazingly, each person who came for this celebration was now hearing the disciples of Jesus speak to them in their own language. Some of those hearing them speaking in their own language made fun of them, accusing them of being drunk. Others, confused, asked one another the meaning of what they were seeing and hearing (Acts 2:1-13).

Peter Teaches On The Christ

So, Peter, the leader of the twelve apostles, stood up with the other eleven apostles and spoke to the mostly Jewish crowd. His purpose for speaking was to convince them Jesus was the Christ, the very one they needed to call on for salvation. Yet they had crucified Jesus with the help of the Romans.

In hearing Peter's accusation and condemnation of having Jesus crucified, they were *"cut to the heart"* and asked Peter what they should do. In recognition of their rejection and crucifixion of the Christ, Peter called for them to repent of what they had done so their sins could be forgiven, then to be baptized in the name of Jesus as a symbol of repentance, of their acceptance of Jesus as the Christ, and of God's forgiveness (Acts 2:14-39).

After recognizing they had crucified their King, thousands of Jewish people repented, believed in Jesus as the Christ, received God's forgiveness, and were baptized (Acts 2:41).

Stephen Before The Sanhedrin

In the early chapters of Acts, the apostles continued to share with Jewish people that Jesus was the Christ. Stephen, a follower of Jesus, also shared that Jesus was the Christ. Stephen, empowered by the Holy Spirit, so boldly spoke of Jesus as the Christ to the people of Israel that he was brought before the ruling powers of Israel, the Sanhedrin.

In the assembly of the Sanhedrin, he was accused of speaking blasphemous words against God and Moses. Then, in the presence of the Sanhedrin, Stephen recounted the history of Israel from Abraham to their present time, concluding the people of Israel had *"betrayed and murdered"* the Righteous One, the Christ.

Upon hearing this accusation and condemnation, the members of the Sanhedrin became *"furious and gnashed their teeth."* At this point, Stephen looked up to heaven, saying he saw Jesus, *"the Son of Man, standing at the right hand of God."* In their anger, the members of the Sanhedrin *"covered their ears and, yelling at the top of their voices, they all rushed at him, dragged him out of the city and began to stone him"* (Acts 6:8-7:60).

What is important to note in the stoning of Stephen is the identity of Saul, the one nodding his head in approval of the stoning. By giving his approval of the stoning, Saul completely rejected Jesus as the Christ (Acts 8:1). Miraculously, the story of God's grace would eventually intersect with the story of Saul's life, and his life would never be the same.

We will see in a later chapter that Saul, the one who was the most furious and angry toward Stephen and who went on a violent, murderous rampage to stop the spread of the message of Jesus as the Christ, became the very one to whom God selected to reveal the details of the story of his grace, appointing him to share the story of grace with people all over the world. But for now, Saul is the one giving approval of the stoning of Stephen and breathing out murderous threats against those believing Jesus is the Christ.

So where are we now with the story of grace? We have seen the King and kingdom promised by God in the Old Testament were announced to Israel by John, Jesus, and his disciples. However, the people of Israel rejected Jesus as the Christ, calling for his crucifixion. Yet Jesus was resurrected and appeared to his followers for a period of forty days, instructing them about the kingdom of God.

Following this forty-day period, he ascended into heaven. Soon, the Holy Spirit empowered his followers to share the message of Jesus being the Christ with those who had traveled to Jerusalem in celebration of Pentecost. Some who heard the message of Jesus believed, yet many rejected the message. Those who did believe experienced tremendous persecution, such as Stephen, by the hands of those who rejected Jesus as the Christ, such as Saul.

Christ Will Return

One thing we have not discussed is that Peter told the people of Israel God would one day send the Christ who would establish God's kingdom on earth, bringing restoration to the world (Acts 3:17-21). When Jesus does return, the nation of Israel will receive him as its King, and God's kingdom of love, peace, joy, gladness, healing, and righteousness will be established on earth! The question is this, "*How can someone be a part of God's kingdom?*"

During Jesus' life on earth, one of the questions people asked, concerning gaining entrance into the coming kingdom, was, "*How righteous does a person have to be to enter into the kingdom of God?*" That's a good question. It is a question that needs to be answered, because the answer affects all of us. Let's take a look at the story of righteousness.

5

The Story Of Righteousness

We have seen the main question the people of Israel asked and debated when Jesus initially came was, *"Is Jesus really the Christ?"* Another important question they asked and debated among themselves was, *"How could one gain entrance into God's kingdom?"*

What Is Required To Live In God's Kingdom?

The Old Testament speaks of those who will one day live forever on earth in God's kingdom and those who will not. It speaks of living in God's kingdom as inheriting the land, or earth. We see in the Old Testament many verses written about inheriting the land. The following verses say it is the righteous, blameless, upright, and meek who will live on the earth in God's eternal kingdom of love, peace, joy, gladness, healing, and righteousness:

> *Lord, who may dwell in your sanctuary? Who may live*
> *on your holy hill? He whose walk is blameless and*
> *who does what is righteous, who speaks the truth*
> *from his heart and has no slander on his tongue, who*
> *does his neighbor no wrong and casts no slur on his*
> *fellow man…*
>
> Psalms 15:1-3

> *The meek will inherit the land.*
>
> Psalm 37:11

...the righteous will inherit the land and dwell in it forever.

Psalm 37:29

For the upright will live in the land, and the blameless will remain in it; but the wicked will be cut off from the land, and the unfaithful will be torn from it.

Proverbs 2:21

The righteous will never be uprooted, but the wicked will not remain in the land.

Proverbs 10:30

Then will all your people be righteous and will possess the land forever.

Isaiah 60:21

Because of these and other verses from the Old Testament, the people of Israel understood it would take righteousness, blamelessness, uprightness, and meekness for one to live in God's eternal kingdom. So, when John, Jesus, and his disciples announced the good news the kingdom of God had arrived, the people began to discuss just how righteous, blameless, upright, and meek one would have to be to enter God's eternal kingdom, for they all wanted to enter and experience his kingdom. However, their major discussion was about how righteous a person needed to be to enter God's kingdom.

How Righteous Does A Person Need To Be?

Righteousness, to the people of Israel, meant obedience to the law, the Ten Commandments (Deuteronomy 6:25). God gave the Ten Commandments to them through Moses. One group committed to seeking righteousness by obedience to the Ten Commandments was the Pharisees.

The Pharisees were a group of religious men whose daily lives revolved around obeying the Ten Commandments. They even created additional laws designed to protect themselves from getting close to breaking God's commandments, then forced these laws on others.

The people of Israel believed the Pharisees met the righteous standards needed to enter God's kingdom. So, when Jesus told the people of Israel their righteousness must exceed the righteousness of the Pharisees and the teachers of the law for entrance into the kingdom of heaven, they were shocked (Matthew 5:20).

The people of Israel could not believe this. They wondered how anyone could be more righteous than the Pharisees and the teachers of the law. The teachers of the law and the Pharisees were considered by the people of Israel the most righteous people on earth. There was no way their righteousness could exceed the righteousness of the Pharisees and the teachers of the law. So, if the righteousness of the teachers of the law and the Pharisees was not enough to enter the kingdom of heaven, then how righteous would a person have to be to enter the kingdom of heaven? Jesus provided the answer to this question in Matthew 5:48:

"Be perfect, therefore, as your heavenly Father is perfect."

Perfect! How could anyone be as perfect as God? That's impossible! There is nothing unloving, unrighteous, unjust, or impure about him. He is full of love, mercy, grace, patience, kindness, and goodness. We all fall short of his perfection. Exactly! This is Jesus' point. Once we see we are imperfect and unrighteous because of sin, we will call upon his grace to enable us to gain entrance into his kingdom. It is at this point the story of his grace intersects with the story of our lives. This is what Jesus wanted them to see...their need for grace! This is what Jesus wants us to see...our need for grace!

Jesus Expounds On The Law And The Prophets
To convince the people of Israel of their need for grace, including the Pharisees and teachers of the law, Jesus expounded on the law. The law is the righteous requirements of the Law of Moses. The major requirement of the law for entrance into the kingdom of God was obedience to Ten Commandments. By expounding on the law, Jesus helped people realize their sin, so they would receive God's grace.

Because Jesus was so full of grace, some thought he was doing away with the righteous requirements of the law and the teachings of the Prophets about the coming of the Christ. When in reality, he came to fulfill them by completely living a righteous life...a perfect life of love! In Matthew 5:17 Jesus said, *"Do not think I have come to abolish the Law or the Prophets; I have not come to abolish them but fulfill them."*

Internal Righteousness Required To Enter God's Kingdom
Not only did Jesus fulfill the righteous requirements of the law by living a perfect life of love, he also fulfilled them by teaching correctly about the extent of righteousness the law required for entrance into the kingdom of heaven. According to Jesus, it was not external

righteousness that was required to enter the kingdom but internal righteousness.

Jesus taught about the internal requirements of the Ten Commandments in the following verses:

> *"You have heard that it was said to the ancients, 'You shall not murder' and 'Whoever shall murder will be liable to the judgment.' But I say to you that everyone being angry with his brother will be liable to the judgment, and whoever shall say to his brother 'Raca,' will be liable to the Sanhedrin. But whoever shall say, 'Fool!' will be liable to the Gehenna of fire."*
>
> Matthew 5:21-22 (Berean Literal Bible)

Again, Jesus says:

> *"You have heard it said, 'Do not commit adultery.' But I tell you that anyone who looks at a woman lustfully has already committed adultery with her in his heart."*
>
> Matthew 5:27-28

So, we see Jesus taught that the righteousness the law required to gain entrance into the kingdom of heaven was internal. To those who thought entering God's kingdom only required the righteousness which came from external obedience to the law, he said the following,

> *"And if your right eye causes you to stumble, pluck it out and cast it from you. For it is better for you that*

one of your members should perish and not that your whole body should be cast into Gehenna. And if your right hand causes you to stumble, cut it off and cast it from you, for it is better for you that one of your members should perish and not that your whole body should depart into Gehenna."

Matthew 5:29-30 (Berean Literal Bible)

What does Jesus mean by "pluck out your right eye" and "cut off your right hand"? With each verse in the Bible, it is vital the meaning is determined by the verse's context. The context of Matthew 5:29-30 centers around the anticipation by the Jewish people of the coming Messiah and the expectation the Messiah would establish God's kingdom on earth.

As we have learned, this anticipation and expectation finds its roots in the Law of Moses and the Prophets who foretold of the coming Messiah and kingdom he would establish (Isaiah 9:6-7; Jeremiah 23:5-6; Daniel 2:44; 7:14).

The people understood from Scripture that righteousness was required to enter Messiah's kingdom. One group of people looking forward to the establishment of the kingdom of God was the Pharisees. The Pharisees sought after righteousness, so they could enter Messiah's kingdom, but it was an external righteousness based upon obedience to the Ten Commandments (Romans 10:1-5).

They attempted to become righteous (innocent, clean, pure) before God through morality and religious activity (Luke 18:9). Through these attempts, they became self-righteous and self-deceived, thinking they achieved the righteousness necessary to enter the kingdom of God. Yet their hearts were unclean and impure, making them guilty before God and disqualifying them from entering the kingdom.

Jesus knew the righteousness needed to enter the kingdom was internal righteousness...an innocent, clean, and pure heart. In leading up to Matthew 5:29-30, Jesus taught it was the "poor in spirit" and "pure in heart" who would enter the kingdom of God. As we will see later in this chapter, the poor in spirit were those who were aware of God's kindness, admitted the sinful condition of their hearts, and accepted the forgiveness of Jesus, thus enabling them to enter the kingdom. Those in this group were the prostitutes and tax collectors (Matthew 21:31-32).

The Pharisees were the very opposite of the "poor in spirit." They were proud in spirit. They were self-righteousness, boasting in their morality and religious activity. They boasted about their obedience to the Ten Commandments and rejected what Jesus told them, which was their hearts were dirty, unclean, and impure, and they had broken the commandments inwardly.

Since the Pharisees mistakenly believed that righteousness and entrance into the kingdom of God was achieved through external behavior, totally rejecting the truth that their hearts were unrighteous, Jesus challenged them on their belief. If they really thought the righteousness needed to enter the kingdom of God was gained through external behavior, then, according to Jesus, it would make sense for them to remove any part of their bodies preventing them from entering the kingdom, such as an impure eye or hand.

Jesus challenged the false belief of the Pharisees when he told them to pluck out the right eye if it was the eye which would cause a person to violate the commandment in the Ten Commandments which said, "Do Not Commit Adultery." He told them to cut off the right hand if it was the impure hand which would cause one to steal and violate the commandment, "Do Not Steal." He could have very easily told the Pharisees to cut out their tongues, so they would not violate the commandment "Do Not Lie" and miss out on the coming kingdom should they lie.

Jesus told them it is better to lose one member of the body rather than perish and miss out on the kingdom of God on earth. The word *perish* during the time of Jesus meant a person would fall under the judgment of God, should they fail to repent, when he purifies the earth by removing the unrighteous from it prior to establishing his kingdom.

Gehenna, which Jesus spoke of, was the place in Jerusalem where bodies, trash, and refuse was burned and removed from earth. Metaphorically speaking, Jesus compared God's judgment to Gehenna when he removes the unrighteous from the earth.

The Pharisees were very familiar with Gehenna and God's purifying judgment to come. Now Jesus was telling them, for the purpose of exposing their own faulty belief system, that if they wanted to live in the kingdom of God and stay out of Gehenna, God's judgment, then pluck out the bad eye and cut off the bad hand if one of these members of the body would make them unrighteous and keep them from entering the kingdom.

Jesus is teaching it is not a bad eye or bad hand that makes a person unrighteous, it is the heart. Through his teaching, Jesus is seeking to convince his Jewish audience, especially the Pharisees, it is internal righteousness that is required to enter the kingdom of God not external righteousness. If external righteousness was required, then, according to Jesus, they should remove whatever part of the body that could possibly make them unrighteous and cause them to be disqualified from entering the kingdom.

Before understanding grace, these two verses perplexed me. I thought many times to myself, *"What is Jesus talking about? What point is he making in saying to pluck out your eye and cut off your hand?"* As I continued to study the Bible, understanding its story, the meaning of these verses became clear. Jesus is taking the belief of those who think external righteous is required for entrance into God's eternal kingdom to its logical conclusion, as I have summarized in the following statement:

> *If you really think the righteousness required for entering into God's eternal kingdom is achieved through external obedience to the Ten Commandments, then pluck out the eye which causes you to sin so you do not see someone, lust after him or her, and commit adultery. Pluck out the eye causing you to covet so you do not covet. If you really think the righteousness required to enter God's eternal kingdom is achieved through external obedience to the law, then cut off the hand which would cause you to steal so you do not steal.*

Obviously, Jesus is not saying for someone to gouge out an eye or cut off a hand. He is showing the Pharisees that if they really believe the righteousness required to enter God's eternal kingdom is achieved through keeping the Ten Commandments externally, then they should do everything in their power to protect themselves from breaking it.

Jesus is saying to those with this mistaken belief, *"Wouldn't it be better for you to go through this life maimed and enter into God's eternal kingdom rather than go into judgment with all your body parts intact? Is keeping any sinful body part during your lifetime on this earth worth missing out on the kingdom of God, since losing those body parts would protect you from breaking the law so that you could enter God's eternal kingdom?*

Only Grace Can Make Us Righteous

Plucking out one's eye or cutting off one's hand can't cleanse a sinful heart. We don't steal because we have an evil hand. We don't lust or covet because we have an evil eye. We steal, lust, and covet because we have sinful hearts. The problem with mankind is not an eye or hand problem. The problem with mankind is a heart problem.

External obedience to the Ten Commandments can't cleanse a sinful heart. A sinful heart can only be cleansed by grace, Jesus' blood poured out for our sins on the cross. Only grace can make an unrighteous person righteous before God.

> *But now a righteousness apart from the law, has been made known, to which the Law and the Prophets testify. This righteousness from God comes by faith in Jesus Christ to all who believe. There is no difference, for all have sinned and fall short of the glory of God, but are justified freely by his grace through the redemption that came by Jesus Christ. God presented him as a sacrifice of atonement* [propitiation, meaning to fully pay the penalty for our sins] *through faith in his blood.*
>
> Romans 3:21-25

We see in these verses that God made known to us the way to become righteous, or clean and innocent before him, apart from obedience to the law, meaning the Ten Commandments. The way to become righteous before God is by his grace, the blood of Jesus poured out for us on the cross where he fully paid the penalty for our sins. By faith, we receive God's gift of grace.

Look at the following verses in Romans 5:15-19.

But the gift [the gift of righteousness by grace] *is not like the trespass* [the sin of Adam spreading to the entire human race], *For if the many* [the entire human race] *died by the trespass of the one man* [Adam], *how much more did God's grace and the gift that came by the grace of the one man, Jesus Christ, overflow to the many* [the entire human race]! *Again, the gift of God is not like the result of the one man's sin: the judgment* [death] *followed one sin and brought condemnation, but the gift* [righteousness through grace] *followed many trespasses and brought justification* [the gracious act of God when he declares a person to be eternally righteous in his sight the moment he places his faith in Jesus' payment for his sins]. *For if, by the trespass of the one man, death reigned through that one man, how much more will those who receive God's abundant provision of grace and the gift of righteousness reign in life through the one man, Jesus Christ. Consequently, just as the trespass of one man was condemnation for all men, so also the result of one act of righteousness* [grace, Jesus' blood poured out for our sins] *was justification that brings life for all men. For just as through the disobedience of the one*

> *man, the many were made sinners, so also through*
> *the obedience of the one man* [Jesus] *the many will*
> *be made righteous.*

These verses teach us that Adam's sin spread to the many, meaning the entire human race, bringing death, condemnation, and judgment. But through Jesus, grace overflowed to the entire human race, bringing justification and righteousness!

It is the obedience of Jesus, meaning his death on the cross for our sins (Philippians 2:8) that makes us righteous before God (2 Corinthians 5:21; 1 Peter 3:18). Rather than trying to make ourselves righteous before God through obedience to the law, we simply receive by faith the abundant provision of grace freely provided for us by God in Jesus. Rather than trying to behave our way into a righteous standing before God, we simply believe in what Jesus has done for us and enjoy the gift of righteousness we have been given.

All I Needed To Do Was Believe!

Understanding this biblical truth set me free to enjoy my relationship with God. For years I thought I had to behave my way into a righteous standing before God. As a result, some days I felt righteous, or accepted by God, and other days I did not. Through my external obedience to religious activities and morality, I was seeking to gain God's acceptance, even though it had already been freely provided for me by God through grace. All I needed to do was believe.

Once, after speaking on grace, someone came up to me and said, *"My entire life I have been trying to behave my way into right standing with God when all I had to do was believe!"* That's it! Just believe!

Religious activities and morality cannot cleanse a sinful heart. This was the point Jesus was making when he talked about a person's righteousness having to exceed that of the Pharisees and teachers of the law to enter God's kingdom.

Jesus' Sermon On The Mount

The section of the Bible where Jesus talks about a person's righteousness having to exceed that of the Pharisees and teachers of the law to gain entrance into the kingdom of God is known as the *Sermon On The Mount*. Jesus, while on the mountainside, not only teaches on the righteous requirements for entering God's kingdom but also on who will enter God's kingdom.

The Poor in Spirit

Jesus began the *Sermon On The Mount* by describing the characteristics of the ones who will enter the kingdom of heaven. He said those who enter the kingdom of heaven are the *poor in spirit* (Matthew 5:3). The poor in spirit are those who repent by recognizing God's kindness. God's kindness leads them to humbly acknowledge to him their spiritual poverty. They acknowledge they have no righteousness. They acknowledge they have broken the Ten Commandments. They acknowledge their immorality. They acknowledge their sin.

By acknowledging their sin, the poor in spirit agree with God they have fallen short of his righteous standard (Romans 3:23). They have fallen short of his glory, his perfect love. They have fallen short of the two great commandments on which all the law and prophets hang. These commandments are loving God with all their heart, soul, mind, and strength, and loving their neighbor as they love themselves (Matthew 22:37-40; Luke 10:25-37).

They have fallen short of loving, praying for, and speaking to their enemies (Matthew 5:38-47). They have fallen short of forgiving others (Matthew 6:12, 14; 18:21-22). They have fallen short by judging others (Matthew 7:1-6). They have fallen short by failing to treat others the way they want to be treated, which, according to Jesus, is what the entire law is all about (Matthew 7:12). They have fallen short of extending grace to their enemies (Luke 6:27-35).

They acknowledge they do not qualify for entrance into God's kingdom because, when putting their hand to the plow and following Jesus' command to never look back, they look back (Luke 9:62). They have fallen short of denying themselves and picking up their cross daily and following Jesus (Luke 9:23). They acknowledge that every day they act selfishly in their thoughts and deeds. They fall short of giving up everything to follow Jesus (Luke 14:33).

They acknowledge there is only One who put his hand to the plow and did not look back, Jesus. They acknowledge there is only one who gave up everything, Jesus. They acknowledge entrance into God's kingdom is not achieved by taking up their cross but is received by faith in the One who took up his cross for them (1 Corinthians 2:2). They acknowledge entrance into God's kingdom is through the cross of Jesus (Galatians 6:14). They acknowledge they fall short of all of Jesus' teachings and commandments. They acknowledge they are spiritually bankrupt and in need of God's grace.

The disciples are great examples of those who fell short, displaying their spiritual bankruptcy and need for grace. They could not fulfill the calling of Jesus to deny themselves, take up their cross, and follow him. What did they do instead? They argued over who would be the most powerful. They argued over what positions they would have in the kingdom. They argued over who would serve them in the kingdom.

Following Jesus' arrest, they all deserted him (Matthew 26:56). Then Peter, who said he would never deny him (Matthew 26:31-35), denied him three times (Luke 22:54-62). His own disciples failed miserably in denying themselves and taking up their cross and following Jesus. Consequently, they became poor in spirit, acknowledging and mourning their sin.

Those Who Mourn

In the *Sermon on the Mount*, Jesus said the poor in spirit mourn (Matthew 5:4). The poor in spirit are broken in their hearts over having disobeyed the Ten Commandments. They are broken in their hearts over having made something more important than God. They are broken in their hearts over having committed adultery and murder, whether internally in their hearts or externally with their deeds. They mourn over lying to others. They mourn over disobeying their parents. They mourn over coveting. They mourn over their immorality. They mourn over their pride. They mourn over their envy and jealousy. They mourn over their judgmental attitude. They mourn over their lack of love for God and others. They are not happy about their sin. They are hurting. They feel shame. They feel guilt. They feel condemned. Yet Jesus says, "*...they will be comforted*" (Matthew 5:4).

How will comfort come to those who are broken and hurting from their sins? Grace! Grace is God's comfort for those who are broken and hurting from their sins (Psalm 51:17; Isaiah 57:15). God longs to pour out his grace on the broken (Isaiah 31:15-18). We see in Jesus' ministry that it was his grace, or his unconditional love, unearned blessings, unmerited kindness, and unlimited forgiveness that brought comfort to those acknowledging their sins and mourning over them.

One example of this is found in Luke 7:36-50 when the *"immoral woman"* enters a Pharisee's house where Jesus is having dinner. Acknowledging her sins and weeping and mourning over them, she falls to her knees behind Jesus, then Jesus comforts her with grace. She received his grace by faith. Jesus told her, *"Your faith has saved you...go in peace"* (Luke 7:50). She came into the Pharisee's house full of shame and condemnation. She left full of grace and forgiveness. When the story of God's grace intersected with the story of her life, comfort came. Her life was never the same.

The Meek

While teaching on the mountainside, Jesus said it is the meek who will inherit the earth (Matthew 5:5), or who will live in God's eternal kingdom of love, peace, joy, gladness, healing, and righteousness. The meek are the poor in spirit and those who mourn. They have been humbled by their sin and carry no pride nor boast in any way about their own righteousness because they know they have none.

They are fully aware of the sins in their heart, mind, and thoughts, as well as their deeds. They know they have fallen short of the righteous requirements of the Ten Commandments in their head (thoughts), heart (desires), and hands (decisions). As a result, they are fully aware they do not qualify to enter the kingdom of heaven. They do not possess the righteousness the law requires. Desperately, they hunger and thirst for righteousness as starving and parched people because they know they have none, and without it, entrance into God's kingdom will not be allowed.

Those Who Hunger And Thirst For Righteousness

Amazingly, Jesus said to this group of people, *"Blessed are those who hunger and thirst for righteousness for they will be filled"* (Matthew 5:6). Suddenly, hope came! Jesus was telling those who had no hope of entering God's kingdom that their desperate desire for righteousness would be filled. He told those hungering and thirsting for righteousness, those who had sinned and fallen short of the righteousness required to enter God's kingdom, that righteousness would be provided. But how? How would the righteousness needed to enter God's eternal kingdom be provided? By grace! God, through his abundant provision of grace, freely offers the gift of righteousness to those who will receive it (Romans 5:17).

As we saw earlier, it is by grace that we are declared righteous by God. We are filled with the righteousness of God by grace through faith. Grace is our only hope of entering God's eternal kingdom. And his grace is available to everybody!

> *For the grace of God that brings salvation has appeared to all men.*
>
> Titus 2:11

The Merciful

On the mountainside, Jesus continued to teach about the kingdom of heaven. He taught that those who show mercy are those who will be given mercy (Matthew 5:7). Those who show mercy are the poor in spirit who have received mercy from God. From mercy freely given to us by God, we give his mercy to others. We do not earn mercy from God by giving mercy, nor do we earn our way into God's kingdom by giving mercy. Rather, we receive mercy from God by humbly realizing our need for mercy and gratefully receiving it by faith. We then give his mercy away, and, in return, are shown mercy by others.

Jesus told a story about a man who stood outside of the temple who prayed, *"God, have mercy on me, a sinner."* While another man, a Pharisee, walked right into the temple and prayed, *"God, I thank you that I am not like other people—robbers, evildoers, adulterers—or even like this tax collector. I fast twice a week and give a tenth of all I get."* Jesus said it was the man who asked for mercy who went home justified, or righteous before God, and was allowed to enter the kingdom of God (Luke 18:9-14).

Ephesians 2:1-5 speaks of the mercy God has shown us in our sin:

> *As for you, you were dead in your transgressions and sins...we were by nature objects of wrath. But because of his great love for us, God, who is rich in mercy, made us alive with Christ even when we were dead in our transgressions - it is by grace you have been saved.*

These verses teach us it is because of God's abundant love, mercy, and grace that we are no longer dead in our sins and objects of wrath (under judgment for our sins). Rather, we have become objects of his love, mercy and grace. As a result, we have been made alive with Christ and have been saved from wrath.

The Pure In Heart

Jesus also teaches in the *Sermon on the Mount* that the pure in heart will see God, or enter God's kingdom (Matthew 5:8).

Remember, the people of Israel thought it was external obedience to the Ten Commandments that secured a place in his kingdom. But Jesus taught internal purity was required. And how are our hearts purified? Again, it is by grace.

Hebrews 1:3 says Jesus provided purification for our sins. By his grace, he tasted death for everyone (Hebrews 2:9). This purification of our sins comes through grace, his shed blood on the cross, which cleanses us from all sin and is received by faith. Because our sins have been cleansed by the blood of Jesus, we draw close to God (Hebrews 7:18-19; 10:22; 1 John 1:7).

The Peacemakers

As Jesus continued to teach on who will enter into God's kingdom, he says it is the peacemakers who will be called sons of God, or loved children of his kingdom (Matthew 5:9). And who are the peacemakers? The peacemakers are those who receive his grace. Jesus was approached by a woman who had lived a very sinful life. This was the same woman written about earlier in the chapter. This woman was so full of guilt and shame that she would not look at him but knelt behind him while weeping. Jesus told this woman her faith had saved her, her sins had been forgiven, and she could go in peace (Luke 7:50). By faith, she received his grace and could live in peace.

Romans 5:1-2 says:

Therefore, since we have been justified through faith,
we have peace with God through our Lord Jesus
Christ, through whom we have gained access by faith
into this grace in which we now stand.

As recipients of God's grace, which is his unconditional love, unearned blessings, unmerited kindness, and unlimited forgiveness, we become peacemakers. Just as God made peace with us through grace, we make peace with others through grace. We freely give to others the grace God has freely given to us. Where grace goes, peace flows!

Ephesians 1:2 says, *"Grace and peace to you from God the Father."* When we experience grace from God, our loving Father, peace flows into our lives. When we begin to share his grace with others, peace flows into their lives.

Persecution Of Grace

Jesus said those who embrace the way of grace as the way to become righteous for entrance into God's kingdom become the salt of the earth and the light of the world, leading to persecution from the religious. (Matthew 5:11-16). Jesus experienced tremendous persecution from the religious for the grace he abundantly poured out on those acknowledging their spiritual poverty, mourning over their sin, and hungering and thirsting for righteousness. The persecution he endured came from the Pharisees. But why? Why would the Pharisees persecute Jesus so harshly?

6

The Story Of The Pharisees

As we saw in the previous chapter, the Pharisees prided themselves in their ability to obey the Ten Commandments. They believed they gained entrance into the kingdom of God through obedience to the law. They felt they were more righteous than everyone else. They bragged about their own righteousness with a very haughty, religious spirit. Rather than being poor in spirit, they were prideful in spirit. Rather than mourning and displaying meekness over their sin, they made themselves the standard of righteousness. Rather than hungering and thirsting for the righteousness they did not have, they were filled with self-righteousness.

As you can imagine, they hated Jesus. They despised him. But why? Because of grace! Jesus was full of the very thing they hated, grace! He told them the truth about their self-righteous condition, which made them hate him even more. The pages of Matthew, Mark, Luke, and John reflect this collision of the self-righteousness of the Pharisees with the righteousness that comes by grace through faith in Jesus. Let's take a closer look at this collision of self-righteousness and grace between the Pharisees and Jesus.

Jesus Reveals God's Grace

John 1:1-2 says *"In the beginning was the Word and the Word was with God and the Word was God...The Word became flesh and made his dwelling among us. We have seen his glory, the glory of the One and Only, who came from the Father full of grace and truth...From the fullness of his grace we have all received one blessing after another. For the law was given through Moses; grace and truth came through Jesus Christ. No one has ever seen God, but God the One and Only, who is at the Father's side, has made him known."*

These verses show us that Jesus, the Word becoming flesh, came to make God known by revealing his grace to the human race. Jesus came to reveal God's unconditional love, unearned blessings, unmerited kindness, and unlimited forgiveness to sinful people. He came to unfold the story of grace in the lives of people who were in desperate need of grace because of their sin. Jesus came so the story of God's grace would intersect with the story of our sinfulness and brokenness, forever changing our lives.

The Word, full of grace and truth, became flesh and lived among sinful, broken people. Through Jesus, one blessing of grace after another came to the human race. Like waves rolling upon the shore, gently, but powerfully, God's grace flowed into the lives of broken people through Jesus, bringing peace by setting them free from guilt, shame, and condemnation. What more could people, humbled and broken by their sin, need than grace? Nothing. Grace was the greatest need of the human race, and Jesus brought grace in abundance!

The Word becoming flesh is such a great way to describe God's heart. Words we speak are an external expression of internal emotions. Words reveal the heart of a person. Jesus, as the Word becoming flesh, came to reveal God's heart, a heart of grace. God revealed his justice through Moses by giving him the law, but through Jesus, he revealed his grace.

The Old Testament foretold that when this Savior-King comes, the Christ, he would reveal God's grace to people. We have already discovered that when the Christ comes, his lips would be anointed with grace (Psalm 45:2). The following verses give us further insight into the graceful disposition of the coming Savior-King and the unfolding of the story of God's grace in the lives of people:

> *"Here is my servant whom I uphold, my chosen one in whom I delight; I will put my Spirit on him, and he will bring justice to the nations. He will not shout or cry out, or raise his voice in the streets. A bruised reed he will not break, and a smoldering wick he will not snuff out…"*
>
> Isaiah 42:1-3; Matthew 12:18-20

Jesus' Healing Words Of Grace

The healing words of grace, describing the coming Savior-King, God's servant, are beautiful in these verses. These verses tell us that when the Christ comes, he will not be loud and harmful but loving and healing. He will not beat people down further with yelling and screaming but will lift people up with gentleness and grace. Very gently, he will bring healing to the bruised and broken and hope to the hopeless.

A bruised reed, illustrating a person who has been beaten and bruised by sin, will find healing through the grace of Jesus. A smoldering wick, illustrating a person who is on the verge of losing all hope because of sin, will find hope through the grace of Jesus.

The Year Of The Lord's Grace

As his grace flows into the hearts of the hurting and hopeless, they will be set free and released from the imprisonment of their pain.

Their eyes will be opened by the beauty of his grace, as these verses indicate:

> *"The Spirit of the Lord is on me, because he has anointed me to preach good news to the poor. He has sent me to proclaim freedom for the prisoners and recovery of sight for the blind, to release the oppressed, to proclaim the year of the Lord's favor…"*
>
> Isaiah 61:1-2

"The year of the Lord's favor" is referring to God's grace when his unconditional love, unearned blessings, unmerited kindness, and unlimited forgiveness are announced by Christ to the poor, or to those who are aware of their unrighteousness and who are hurting from their sin. It refers to a time when God's grace is announced to those imprisoned by guilt, shame, and condemnation, to those who can't see any way out of the darkness of their broken and hopeless condition, and to those who are oppressed and tormented with regret because of all they have done.

When Christ announces the good news of God's grace to the hurting, condemned, broken, hopeless, and tormented, then freedom, hope, joy, and peace will come. As people see the beauty of God's grace through the gentleness of Christ, chains will be broken, hope will be restored, and peace will come. Guilt, shame, and condemnation will be replaced with freedom and joy.

At the age of thirty, when attending his childhood synagogue in Nazareth, Jesus read Isaiah 61:1-2 to the congregation (Luke 4:16-21). After reading these verses, he said, *"Today this scripture is fulfilled in your hearing."* Jesus was declaring he was the one whom Isaiah said was to come and announce the time of God's grace.

The people initially responded by speaking well of him and were *"amazed at the gracious words that came from his lips"* (Luke 4:22). Not only were these verses fulfilled in the presence of those listening to Jesus read from Isaiah, but they were also fulfilled in the lives of all the hurting, broken, condemned, hopeless, and tormented people whose life story intersected with the story of God's grace.

The Pharisees' Hatred For Grace

It was this abundance of grace flowing from Jesus into the lives of sinful people that angered the Pharisees so much. Again, the Pharisees and the teachers of the law prided themselves on the mistaken belief that since they had obeyed the Ten Commandments, they had gained entrance into the kingdom of God. They did not see their own sinfulness and unrighteousness. They did not see their need for grace. All they saw was their own self-righteousness. Mourning over sin? Never! Bragging about their righteousness? Always!

In glorying in their own self-righteousness, *"they looked down on everyone else"* (Luke 18:9). In their feelings of righteous superiority, they constantly criticized Jesus for spending time with "sinners". They delighted in calling people "sinners". Calling people "sinners" made them feel even more superior. Matthew, Mark, Luke, and John quite often put the word sinners in quotations because they were quoting the Pharisees' description of those they deemed unrighteous.

Jesus had a heart of love for the sinners which the Pharisees hated. He spent large amounts of time with them. The Pharisees would often ask Jesus' disciples why he spent time with "sinners" (Matthew 9:11). Because Jesus spent so much time with sinful people, the Pharisees called him *"a friend of tax collectors and sinners*" (Matthew 11:19) *"who welcomes "sinners" and eats with them"* (Luke 15:2).

Even though the Pharisees used these descriptions of Jesus as derogatory terms, these descriptions wonderfully describe how graceful Jesus was to those living a sinful life. Through these descriptions, we see the heart of Jesus to connect the story of God's grace with the story of the lives of sinners, which put him on a collision course with the Pharisees!

The Pharisees, Jesus, And A Woman Caught In Adultery (John 8:2-11)

This collision of law and grace between the Pharisees and Jesus was a normal part of Jesus' life. One morning, Jesus was teaching in front of a crowd that had gathered to hear him. In an attempt to trap Jesus between the Law of Moses and grace, the Pharisees dragged a woman they caught in the act of adultery into the presence of Jesus. Making her stand before the group, they told Jesus the Law of Moses commanded she be stoned to death. They wanted to know what he thought about this commandment. Would he extend grace to her or would he consent to stoning her as the Law of Moses required?

Jesus always replied masterfully to the Pharisees. In this case, he said whoever was without sin, let him be the first one to cast a stone at the woman. Before saying this, Jesus started writing on the ground. Whatever he wrote made the Pharisees leave one by one. So, the question is, what did he write?

Because each Pharisee left one by one as Jesus was writing on the ground, and because Jesus said let he who is without sin cast the first stone, it is highly possible he was writing the sins of each man. As the Pharisees' sins were exposed to the crowd, they left one by one until only Jesus remained.

Jesus was the only one in the crowd without sin and who could rightfully cast a stone at her. However, Jesus poured grace upon her rather than casting a stone at her. He poured upon her unconditional love, unearned blessings, unmerited kindness, and unlimited forgiveness. As she experienced his grace, he told her to leave her life of sin. Because she had experienced grace in her sin, she was empowered to leave her life of sin.

Even though Jesus was gentle and humble in heart (Matthew 11:29) and full of grace, he was very direct with the Pharisees, reserving his harshest words for them. The Bible tells us Jesus was not only full of grace but also full of truth (John 1:14). Many say, in pointing to John 1:14, that grace must be balanced with truth, as if grace is not truth. Grace does not need to be balanced with anything because grace is the power of God to change a person's life. The truth referred to here is the truth Jesus shared directly with the Pharisees, truthfully confronting them of their erroneous beliefs, teachings, and self-righteousness (Matthew 23:28).

Many times when speaking to the Pharisees about their self-righteousness, Jesus would say, *"I tell you the truth."* In telling them the truth, he called them *"hypocrites"* (Matthew 23:23), *"blind guides"* (Matthew 23:24), and *"liars"* (John 8:55). He called them *"snakes"* and a *"brood of vipers"* who were on the verge of judgment. He asked them how they would escape judgment (Matthew 23:33). Little did they know it was the very grace they hated that would allow them to escape the judgment to come. Yet they did not see their need for grace. They thought they were already citizens of the kingdom of God because of their own righteousness.

Jesus had other harsh words for the Pharisees. He said they and other religious leaders belonged *"to your father, the devil"* (John 8:44). He accused them of placing heavy demands on people, demands they themselves could not keep (Matthew 23:1-4). He accused them of parading around in front of people, seeking the praise of men (Matthew 23:5-7). He cautioned his disciples against allowing the dangerous teachings of the Pharisees to influence them (Matthew 16:5-12). Jesus definitely did not shy away from speaking the truth to the Pharisees about their self-righteousness.

Jesus' Stories Of Grace

To confront this attitude of self-righteousness in the Pharisees, their hatred for grace, and the time he spent with sinners, Jesus often told stories or parables.

The Story Of The Father's Grace

One story Jesus told to illustrate the Pharisees' hatred of his grace toward sinners was about a man who had two sons, a younger son and an older son. This story is found in Luke 15:11-31 and is commonly known as *The Story of the Prodigal Son*.

In this story, the younger son represents the sinners, whom the Pharisees despised but to whom Jesus dispensed grace. The older son represents the self-righteous attitude of the Pharisees and their anger toward God for the grace he freely gave to sinners through Jesus.

The story goes like this: The younger brother travels far away from home and spends all his inheritance in wild, sinful living. After blowing all his money by indulging in this extremely sinful lifestyle, the younger brother found himself with no money, no food, in a pig pen, and starving to death. He was overcome with guilt and shame. To say the least, he was miserable...beyond miserable!

While in this condition, he remembered that on his father's farm the hired servants had plenty of food to eat. So, he devised a plan to earn his way back into his father's heart and home and decided he would return home. The plan he devised was this: he would tell his father he had sinned against heaven and his father and that he was no longer worthy to be called his father's son. After his confession, he would ask his father to allow him to work on the farm as a hired servant. He started the long journey home, rehearsing his plan with each step.

Every day his father would wake up, look down the long dusty road leading away from home, and say, "*Is this the day my son comes home?*". But day after day after day after day...no son. Then, one day, he looked down the road, and there, far away in the distance, was his son coming home. Filled with compassion (mercy), he ran to his son, put his arms around him, and kissed him. The son told his father he had sinned against heaven and his father, and he was no longer worthy to be called his son. But the father responded quickly by having the best robe in the house brought to his son and the fattened calf in the field prepared for a party he would throw in celebration of his son's return. The story of grace had intersected the story of the younger brother's life!

And celebrate they did! With dancing and music, they celebrated. This act of grace on the father's part infuriated the older brother. He refused to join in the celebration of his younger brother's return. He lashed out at his father, telling him he had been slaving away for years in obedience to his father's commands but never receiving a party. And now a party is thrown for his rebellious, undeserving younger brother. If anyone deserved a party, the older brother thought, it would be him, not his sinful younger brother!

This story is a perfect example of how Jesus lavished grace upon the sinners the Pharisees despised and how the Pharisees loathed the grace Jesus lavished upon them. It demonstrates the actual feelings of the Pharisees toward God.

Jesus revealed the heart of the Pharisees through the older brother when the older brother said he had been slaving away for many years obeying his father's commands. Their approach to God was one of a slave to a slave owner. To them, God was a slave master who must be appeased through strict obedience to the Ten Commandments. The ultimate reward for their obedience would be entrance into God's kingdom.

In the minds of the Pharisees, they had been slaving away for many years in obedience to the Ten Commandments, thinking they had earned their way into his kingdom. Therefore, they were furious with the grace Jesus poured upon the rebellious, disobedient "sinners" who gained entrance into God's kingdom simply by grace through faith. There was no way they were going to celebrate the grace Jesus lavished on these "sinners" and attend a grace party...absolutely not!

Little did they realize, however, they were just as disobedient to the Ten Commandments internally as were the "sinners" externally. They, too, needed God's grace, the very grace they hated, to enter the kingdom.

Jesus called the Pharisees *"whitewashed tombs"* (Matthew 23:27) and *"cups that were clean on the outside but filthy on the inside"* (Matthew 23:25), meaning, they looked very clean on the outside but were rotten and dirty on the inside.

The Story Of The Pharisee And The Tax Collector

Another story Jesus told to confront the self-righteousness of the Pharisees was about two men who went up to the temple to pray (Luke 18:9-14). One of the men was a Pharisee and the other a tax collector. The Pharisee went into the temple to pray. His prayer consisted of boasting about his own righteousness and thanking God he was not like the unrighteous.

The tax collector, however, would not even go into the temple or look up to heaven. Standing at a distance, with his head hanging low in humility, shame, guilt, and condemnation, and admitting he was a sinner, he asked for mercy from God. Jesus then said the man who went home justified, or righteous in God's sight, was the tax collector, not the Pharisee.

The story of God's grace had intersected with the story of this broken and humble tax collector but not with the story of the Pharisee's. This was because the Pharisee did not see his need for grace, but the humble tax collector did.

As these stories indicate, the Pharisees never saw their sinfulness and unrighteousness. It was people like the prostitutes and the tax collectors who saw their own sinfulness and unrighteousness. In seeing their own sinfulness and unrighteousness, they admitted their spiritual poverty, mourned over it, hungered and thirsted for righteousness, and were filled with the righteousness that came by grace through faith in Jesus. Therefore, because they received the righteousness that came by grace through faith, they were able to enter the kingdom of God, whereas the Pharisees could not.

Concerning the tax collectors and prostitutes entering the kingdom of God rather than the Pharisees, Jesus said the following to the chief priests and the elders of the people, which would have included the Pharisees:

> *"I tell you the truth, the tax collectors and the
> prostitutes are entering the kingdom of God ahead of
> you* [Pharisees]. *For John came to show you the way*

of righteousness [believing in Jesus as the Christ]*, and
you did not believe him* [believe Jesus is the Christ]*,
but the tax collectors and the prostitutes did. And
even after you saw this, you did not repent* [admit
your sinful and unrighteous condition to God and
accept his grace] *and believe him* [believe Jesus was
the Christ].

Matthew 21:31-32

The fact that Jesus said tax collectors and prostitutes were entering the kingdom of God ahead of the Pharisees angered the Pharisees. They could not believe what they were hearing from Jesus. So, they made it their goal to get rid of him.

The Story Of The Good Samaritan

The Story of the Good Samaritan, found in Luke 10:25-37, is often taught by Pastors and Bible teachers to motivate their church to "Love your neighbor as yourself" by doing good deeds as the Good Samaritan did. In teaching this, they totally miss the context of the story and the reason Jesus told the story.

Jesus' purpose in telling this story was not to get the average church member to do good deeds. His purpose was to confront the self-righteousness of an expert in the law, most likely a Pharisee, who asked him a question.

The expert in the law asked Jesus what he must do to inherit eternal life, meaning to live forever in the kingdom of God. He asked this to test Jesus. He did not really want to know the answer to his question, but he wanted to see how Jesus would answer the question, hoping Jesus would downplay the law as the standard of righteousness a person must meet to gain eternal life.

Jesus answered the man's question by asking a question. He asked the expert in the law what the law said a person must do to inherit eternal life. The man answered by quoting the law's two great commandments: *"Love the Lord your God with all your heart, all your soul, all your strength, and all your mind"* and *"Love your neighbor as you love yourself."* Jesus replied to him, telling him *"Do this and you will live."*

The expert in the law then asked Jesus another question. He asked Jesus who is a person's neighbor. To answer this man's question, Jesus tells a story about good Samaritan. This story is directed specifically at the expert in the law to confront his self-righteousness because this man was confident he had obeyed the two great commandments and was deserving of eternal life. In this story, Jesus demonstrates to the expert that he had not loved his neighbor as he loved himself, and as a result, had not loved God with all his heart, all his soul, all his strength, and all his mind; thus, disqualifying him entrance into God's eternal kingdom.

The story consists of four men and some thieves. The thieves had stripped, beat, and robbed a man, leaving him on the road to die. Two men, one a priest and the other a Levi, passed by the man, noticing but not helping him. Another man, a Samaritan, helped the man. Jesus then asked the expert which one of the men in the story was a neighbor to the one who had been robbed. The expert said it was the man who did good. Jesus then told the expert in the law to do as the Samaritan did to gain eternal life. This was shocking to the expert in the law because he hated the Samaritan. He hated him so much that he could not even say the word "Samaritan" in the story, only referring to him as "the one who did good".

Now Jesus is telling the expert in the law to love like the one he hates. In doing this, Jesus reveals to the man that he had broken the two great commandments by having hate in his heart toward the Samaritan.

In context, we see the purpose of the story was to convince the expert in the law of his inability to obey the two great commandments: "Love the Lord your God with all your heart, all your soul, all your strength, and all your mind" and "Love your neighbor as you love yourself." And by doing so, to convince the man of his need for grace to enter the kingdom of God...the same grace the prostitutes and the tax collectors needed.

Not only could the expert in the law not obey the two great commandments, none of us can. As we learned in chapter five, none of us can love God with all our heart, all our soul, all our strength, and all our mind, nor can we love our neighbor as we love ourselves. That is the point of Jesus' story of the good Samaritan. We are all in need of grace to enter God's kingdom.

The Story Of The King's Grace

There is one more story I would like to share with you, it is commonly called *The Story of the Wedding Banquet*. It is about a King's grace.

In this story, a king invited certain people to the wedding banquet he was throwing in honor of his son's marriage. Yet they rejected his invitation. So the king invited everyone in the community to the banquet, both good and bad. Soon the wedding hall was filled with guests who had accepted the invitation. Yet there was one in the wedding hall wearing his own wedding clothes instead of the wedding clothes provided by the king. This guest was tossed out of the banquet into the darkness where there was weeping and gnashing of teeth (Matthew 22:1-14).

The meaning of the story is as follows: God had invited the Pharisees and other religious leaders into his kingdom, but they rejected his invitation by rejecting Jesus as the Christ, the Savior-King. Then God, through grace, invited everyone into his kingdom, providing the wedding clothes of Jesus' righteousness to all those who accepted the invitation of grace. By accepting his gift of righteousness, they gained entrance into his kingdom and ate from the table of grace...the table of unconditional love, unearned blessings, unmerited kindness, and unlimited forgiveness.

Those eating from the table of grace are the prostitutes, tax collectors, and everyone else humbled and broken by their sinfulness. The poor in spirit were feasting from the riches of the table of grace. The one at the wedding banquet not dressed in the proper wedding clothes, but rather his own wedding clothes, represents the Pharisees who dressed themselves in their own wedding clothes of self-righteousness instead of being clothed in the wedding clothes of Christ's righteousness. The Pharisees and other religious leaders were removed from the kingdom of God and tossed into darkness where they wept and gnashed their teeth.

One of these Pharisees attempting to get into God's kingdom dressed in the wedding clothes of his own self-righteousness was a man named Saul. You remember Saul...we mentioned him in chapter four. Saul was the one who gave approval of the stoning of Stephen (Acts 8:1) and was the one at whose feet those stoning Stephen placed their clothes Acts (7:58).

As a Pharisee (Acts 26:5), Saul hated Jesus. He hated grace. But soon, the story of God's grace would intersect with the story of Saul's life, and his life would never be the same. This one-time Pharisee would become the very one to whom the ascended Jesus would reveal the transforming truths of God's grace and who would then reveal these truths to the world!

7

The Story Of Paul

This man named Saul, also known as Paul, would be at the top of the list if we were to rank the Pharisees in order of self-righteousness. Before he placed his faith in Jesus, he prided himself on his religious activity and morality. He prided himself on his obedience to the Law of Moses (Philippians 3:4-6). He was the epitome of self-righteousness, much like the older brother in the previous chapter, enraged at grace and infuriated with Jesus.

Paul's Rampage Of Terror

Along with the other Pharisees, Paul was awaiting the coming Savior-King. Like most of the other Pharisees, he was convinced he did not need a Savior, just a king. When Jesus came, he believed Jesus was an imposter. To Paul, Jesus was definitely not the coming king. So, when thousands of Jews began placing their faith in Jesus as the Savior-King, following the resurrection of Jesus, he went on a violent rampage of terror to eradicate this Jesus movement from the face of the earth (Acts 26:9-12).

Paul, breathing out murderous threats (Acts 9:1), would storm into synagogues where many who had accepted Jesus as the Christ were gathered. With children screaming, he would drag mothers and fathers from these synagogues, taking them away for imprisonment, punishment, and death. As a result, Paul became greatly feared in the Jewish community. The people were terrified of him, wondering if their families or synagogues would be next!

Paul's Revelation Of Grace

Even though Paul fervently sought to eradicate the Jesus movement, it continued to spread, reaching as far as Damascus (Acts 22:2-5). Enraged, Paul set off for Damascus. While on this violent rampage to Damascus, suddenly a bright light from heaven appeared. Paul described this light as *"brighter than the sun"* (Acts 26:13). When this bright light appeared, Paul fell to the ground. A voice spoke to him saying, *"Saul, Saul, why do you persecute me?"* Paul replied, *"Who are you, Lord?"* Then the Lord said, *"I am Jesus whom you are persecuting?"* Jesus then instructed Paul to stand up, telling him he had been appointed to be a servant and a spokesperson of all he had seen, heard, and would be shown (Acts 26:12-18).

Paul described this moment as the time when the story of God's grace intersected with the story of his life, serving as an example to all people that God's grace is available to them no matter who they are or what they have done:

> *"I thank Christ Jesus our Lord, who has given me*
> *strength, that he considered me faithful, appointing*
> *me to his service. Even though I was once a*
> *blasphemer and a persecutor and a violent man, I*
> *was shown mercy because I acted in ignorance. The*
> *grace of our Lord was poured out on me abundantly,*
> *along with the faith and love that are in Christ Jesus.*
> *Here is a trustworthy saying that deserves full*
> *acceptance: Christ Jesus came into the world to save*
> *sinners - of whom I am the worst. But for that very*
> *reason, I was shown mercy so that in me, the worst of*
> *sinners, Christ Jesus might display his unlimited*
> *patience as an example for those who would believe*

on him and receive eternal life. Now to the King
eternal, immortal, invisible, the only God, be honor
and glory for ever and ever. Amen."

1 Timothy 1:12-17

Following this life-changing encounter, Jesus revealed to Paul the truths of God's grace and assigned to him the task of sharing grace with others (Acts 20:24). Paul called the good news of grace the gospel of God's grace. That is because the word gospel means good news. God's grace is good news!

"However, I consider my life worth nothing to me, if I
only may finish the race and complete the task the
Lord has given me - the task of testifying to the
gospel of God's grace."

Acts 20:24

Concerning the revelation of grace given to him by Jesus, Paul said in Galatians 1:11-12, "*I want you to know, brothers, that the gospel I preach is not something that man made up. I did not receive it from any man, nor was I taught it; rather, I received it by revelation from Jesus Christ.*" After his ascension into heaven, Jesus Christ personally revealed to Paul the deeper truths of grace about all he had done for humanity through his life, death, burial, resurrection, and ascension.

Jesus had taken this self-righteous, Jesus-hating, grace-hating Pharisee, who was the leader of a violent movement to remove the name of Jesus and his grace from the face of the earth, and transformed him into the leader of the grace movement by revealing to him the good news of God's grace. What a transformation!
Righteousness Comes By Grace Through Faith

It was through this revelation of grace from Jesus that Paul learned righteousness does not come through obedience to the law but through grace. In Galatians 2:21 Paul says, "*I do not set aside the grace of God, for if righteousness could be gained through the law, then Christ died for nothing!*" He also says in Philippians 3:2-9 that his attempts to become righteous before God through obedience to the law were useless. This one-time, hardcore Pharisee had now come to understand it is only by grace through faith in Jesus that one becomes righteous before God.

This is the truth I learned while reading *Classic Christianity*. For years I had been trying to earn righteousness, or acceptance with God, through religious activity and morality, yet feeling like I could never measure up. However, as I read *Classic Christianity*, I realized that righteousness does not come through my own religious activity or morality but is by grace through faith alone.

Paul learned this truth while riding on a horse from Jerusalem to Damascus. I learned this truth while flying on a plane from Denver to Mobile. For you, maybe right now, wherever you are, the story of God's grace is intersecting with the story of your life, and you are learning that righteousness is not achieved by religious activity or morality but is received by grace through faith in Jesus alone.

Paul's Revolution Of Grace

With this revelation of grace to Paul, a grace movement had begun! Compelled by grace, Paul's one passion was to share the good news of God's grace with as many people as possible. Nothing was more important to Paul than sharing this good news... not even his own life (Acts 20:24).

Because God's grace had totally transformed Paul's life, he would do anything to share the good news of God's grace with others.

He was passionate about reaching more and more people with the transforming truths of grace (2 Corinthians 4:15). He wanted others to experience God's unconditional love, unearned blessings, unmerited kindness, and unlimited forgiveness. Nothing could stop him from sharing grace with others.

Paul went through extremely difficult situations and circumstances to deliver the treasure of grace to people (2 Corinthians 4:7-16). As Paul reached more and more people with God's grace, they began thanking God for his grace poured upon them through Jesus.

Through grace, many people began to realize how great God is! Because of the passionate perseverance of Paul, the story of God's grace intersected with the story of their lives, forever changing their lives, just as it changed Paul's.

In 2 Corinthians 4:15, Paul writes about the transforming impact of God's grace upon people and their gratitude for his grace. He writes, *"All this is for your benefit, so that the grace that is reaching more and more people may result in thanksgiving overflowing to the glory of God."*

Paul's Persecution Because Of Grace

Even though it was worth it, sharing this life-changing message of grace wasn't easy for Paul. In addition to the obstacles he had to overcome, he encountered much persecution from the Pharisees and other religious leaders, but he did not allow any of these people or obstacles to slow him down. Sharing grace was what he was born to do!

Paul says, in Galatians 1:15-16, he was set aside by God in his mother's womb for the specific purpose of sharing grace with people. And share grace he did. With a passionate heart and a persevering spirit, Paul went from city to city sharing God's grace. In many of these cities, he was met with strong opposition to the good news of grace. (Acts 9:29; 13:43-50; 14:3-7; 9-21; 1 Thessalonians 2:4; 2 Timothy 4:14-15). Some opposing his message tried to kill him. However, despite strong opposition, Paul continued to share grace with as many people as possible.

You're Giving People A License to Sin

As Paul continued to share the good news of grace, he was slandered by those opposing his message. The greatest verbal attack upon Paul by those opposing his message was the accusation his teaching of grace was a license for people to sin. They accused Paul of telling people they could sin all they wanted because, according to their misunderstanding of what Paul taught, the more they sinned the more grace God gave.

Paul responded to this accusation in Romans 3:5-8 by stating emphatically:

> *"Why not say - as we are being slanderously reported*
> *as saying and as some claim that we say - 'Let us do*
> *evil* [sin more] *that good* [receive more grace from
> God and praise for God] *may result?'. Their* [those
> who slandered him for teaching grace] *condemnation*
> *is deserved."*

If anyone understood the gospel of grace it was Paul. He had received it directly from the ascended Jesus. So those accusing Paul of giving people a license to sin were not only making this accusation against Paul but against Jesus himself!

This same accusation of giving people a license to sin is made toward teachers of grace today by others who claim to preach the gospel. I have been accused of this many times.

It is unbelievable how people who claim to preach the gospel have so little understanding of the gospel they claim to preach. If they really understood the gospel, the last thing they would do is make this kind of absurd accusation against grace teachers. Just as Paul stated, *"Their condemnation is deserved"* (Romans 3:8).

The accusation against grace teachers is that teaching grace will give people a license to sin. This would be like accusing someone who rescues a person lost in the wilderness of giving them a license to continue to live lost in the wilderness. The lost person's greatest desire is to be rescued, provided food and water, and reunited with his family. Those making this accusation believe this lost person would willingly choose to set off for the wilderness again, even though he has been found, nourished and reunited with his family, and possessing a deep appreciation for the one who rescued him. Absurd? Absolutely!

The truth is the last thing he would want to do is go back into the miserable conditions of wilderness after he has been reunited with his family. This lost one who experienced rescue and restoration will never be the same again.

In this illustration, we see the absurdity of those making this slanderous accusation against grace teachers. Those slandering and accusing grace teachers of giving those who are spiritually lost, hungry, and thirsty a license to sin by sharing the grace freely provided through Jesus to rescue them is unbelievable.

According to those making this ridiculous accusation, the person who desperately desires a relationship with God but is spiritually lost, wandering in the wilderness of sin, shame, guilt, and condemnation, will accept the free offer of grace and then walk back into the wilderness of sin, shame, guilt, and condemnation, rejecting God and showing no appreciation for Jesus, the one who rescued him. That is absurd!

The person aware of his lost condition spiritually, weary from wandering in the wilderness of his sin, shame, guilt, and condemnation, and hungering and thirsting to be filled with God's love and forgiveness, is filled with joy when told about God's unconditional love, unearned blessings, unmerited kindness, and unlimited forgiveness in Jesus. Grace is like a cup of cool water and slice of warm bread to the one lost in the wilderness of sin, drawing him close to Jesus. Isn't this what Jesus is, the water of life to the thirsty and the bread of life to the hungry?

This free offer of grace is made in Revelation 22:17, *"Whoever is thirsty, let him come; whoever wishes, let him take of the free gift of the water of life."* Maybe this is you. You are hungry and thirsty. You have been wandering in the wilderness of your sin, shame, guilt, and condemnation. Jesus offers for you to come drink freely of his grace, to drink of his unconditional love, unearned blessings, unmerited kindness, and unlimited forgiveness.

Grace Fills Our Hearts With Joy

For years, I have seen the good news of grace fill the hearts of many with joy and gratitude who were at one time wandering in the wilderness of their sin, shame, guilt, and condemnation. One of these was Ted.

Ted had been wandering in his personal wilderness of sin, shame, guilt and condemnation for years. For several weeks, he attended my classes on grace but still wandered in his wilderness. Then, one morning, he came up to me with joy bursting from his heart and tears flowing from his eyes saying, *"Thank you so much for teaching me about grace. I thought I could never be close to God again. But because of grace, I realize I can draw close to God."*

Days later, before an audience of over one-hundred people, I watched him share with tears flowing down his face about the power of God's grace delivering him from his sin, shame, guilt, and condemnation, and drawing him close to God in a love relationship. The story of God's grace intersected with the story of Ted's life, and his life has never been the same!

Paul's Persistence In Sharing Grace

Now, let's move back to Paul. Despite strong opposition and verbal accusations toward him and the good news of God's grace, Paul was persistent in telling others about God's grace, not giving in to any of his accusers (Galatians 2:5).

Persistence in the face of opposition and accusations is required if the good news of God's grace is to be shared. In the December 2014 issue of Bob George's newsletter, a letter sent to Bob, thanking him for his persistence in sharing grace, was shared. It stated:

"I first learned of Bob in the late 80's listening to the radio; and came across this guy saying things at first, [that] didn't make sense. And that was because I was so used to hearing the regular stuff all my life. But gradually, as I kept listening, I started saying to myself, "That's right, what he is saying is right." In fact, you [Bob] started to answer all the questions I had stored up all those years listening to the regular stuff, that they could never answer, and really

contradicted the Word that I was reading. Probably for me, the most profound statement for me at that time was: "God gives grace to the humble, but resists the proud." I was coming from a place of utter humility, couldn't get any lower than where I was at. Suicide was a thought, but didn't have the guts. [I was] certainly in a place to receive the understanding of the Grace of God...Thank you for being so instrumental in bringing this sheep back to the Shepherd."

Bob, during his teaching ministry about grace, was often accused of giving people a license to sin. However, because of his persistence in the face of opposition and accusations, people's lives were changed, such as my own, and the one who wrote this letter. Thank you, Bob.

A friend of mine drove home the necessity of being persistent in teaching grace in the face of opposition and accusations when he told me, *"Thank you for being persistent in teaching grace. It took me three months to get it, but because of your persistence in the face of verbal persecution, my life was changed!"*

Paul Asks For Prayer In Sharing Grace

To continue to spread God's grace effectively in the face of opposition and accusations, Paul asked for the prayerful support of those who had already responded to the good news. He asked them to pray for increased opportunities for him to share grace, and, when those opportunities came, he asked them to pray that he would share it fearlessly and clearly.

In Ephesians 6:19-21 Paul writes, *"Pray also for me, that whenever I open my mouth, words may be given me so I will fearlessly make known the mystery of the gospel for which I am an ambassador in chains. Pray that I may proclaim it fearlessly, as I should."* In Colossians 4:3-4 Paul writes, *"And pray for us, too, that God may open a door for our message, so that we may proclaim the mystery of Christ, for which I am in chains. Pray that I may proclaim it clearly, as I should."*

Paul's Debate About Grace

Taking advantage of the opportunities provided by God, Paul fearlessly and clearly shared the message of grace with many people. However, as you can imagine, the message he shared brought him into sharp debate with the Pharisees and other religious leaders. In Acts 13:23-37, Paul told the Jewish people that Jesus was the Savior-King God promised in the Old Testament. Furthermore, he told them it was through faith in Jesus, not following the Law of Moses, that a person received God's forgiveness and was justified, or declared accepted by God (Acts 13:38-39). It was this teaching that brought sharp debate between Paul and the Pharisees (Acts 15:2).

As the message of Jesus being the Christ spread, some of the Pharisees came to faith in Jesus. However, many of them simply added Jesus to the Law of Moses, stating for one to be truly saved, or declared righteous before God, they not only had to place their faith in Jesus, but they also had to follow the Mosaic Law. They even told the Gentiles (non-Jewish people) that to be saved they must first convert to Judaism.

After much debate and discussion, Peter, the disciple of Jesus, stood up and said converting to Judaism and obeying the Law of Moses was not required for salvation. According to Peter, no one could obey the Law of Moses. Attempting to have people obey it for salvation would be going against the message of God's grace and against God himself. Peter proclaimed that salvation was through the grace of Jesus Christ (Acts 15:1-11).

Paul Established Grace-Based Churches

The purpose of Paul's travels from city to city was not only to share the good news of God's grace with people but also to start grace-based churches consisting of those who responded to his message. He was very strategic in doing this (1 Corinthians 9:19-23). Paul became an expert builder in establishing churches whose foundation was grace (1 Corinthians 3:10). Establishing grace-based churches was the strategy given to Paul by the ascended Jesus for the purpose of becoming communication and education centers of God's grace to the people in these cities.

Once established, Paul would appoint a church leadership team of pastors, teachers, overseers, and elders to lead the church (Acts 14:23, Titus 1:5) and carry out its mission of sharing grace and to protect its message of grace.

The Church In Ephesus

One church Paul established was the church in Ephesus (Acts 18:19-21; 19). The church in Ephesus was a grace-centered church (Ephesians 1-3). He taught the people about grace publicly and from house to house (Acts 20:17-20). Also, Paul wrote a letter to the Ephesian church to further teach and establish them in the truths of grace. In the Bible, this letter is known as Ephesians.

Paul met with the leaders of the church in Ephesus, warning them non-grace people, savage wolves as Paul called them, would come into the church and prey on the grace-believers. These savage wolves would seek to devour them by ripping the good news of grace from them and placing them back under the law. Some of these savage wolves would come from right inside the church (Acts 20:17-32).

The Church In Thessalonica

Another church Paul established was in Thessalonica. When the story of God's grace intersected with the lives of those in Thessalonica, their lives were never the same. Paul said the Thessalonian people welcomed with joy the message of grace. Soon this church became a model for surrounding churches of proclaiming the good news of God's grace in their own cities (1 Thessalonians 1:4-8, 13).

The Church In Colossae

Colossae was another city where a grace-based church was established. Epaphras, a companion of Paul, started this church when he began sharing God's grace in this city. The truth of God's grace had such an impact on the people that it totally changed their lives the very day they heard and understood it!

Colossians 1:3-8 says:

We always thank God, the Father of our Lord Jesus
Christ, when we pray for you because we have heard
of your faith in Christ Jesus and of the love you have
for all the saints - the faith and love that spring from
the hope that is stored up for you in heaven and that
you have already heard about in the word of truth,
the gospel that has come to you. All over the world,
this gospel is bearing fruit and growing, just as it has

*been doing among you since **the day you heard it and understood God's grace in all its truth**. You learned it from Epaphras, our dear fellow servant, who is a faithful minister of Christ…*

In these verses, we see the life-changing impact of the truth of grace on the Colossians the moment they understood it. Grace produced faith, hope, love, and fruit in their lives.

Not only did grace produce life-change in the people in Colossae, but grace produced life-change in people all over the world! This is God's heart. He desires for the good news of his grace to be proclaimed to people all over the world, producing life-change the very moment people hear and understand his grace in all its truth.

This is what happened to me! The moment I understood grace in all its truth, my life was immediately changed. Faith, hope, love, and joy immediately flooded my heart while flying in an airplane. Just as the people in Colossae learned the truth of God's grace from Epaphras, I learned it from Bob George while reading *Classic Christianity*.

God doesn't care who we learn about grace from, he just wants us to learn it. Why? Because he wants our lives to be filled with faith, hope, love, and joy. He wants us to experience life-change!

Your Class On Grace Changed My Life!

Several years ago, I was teaching a one-hour class on grace. Immediately after class, someone approached me and said, *"Your class on grace has changed my life! I have learned more about the Bible in this class than all the sermons, small groups, and Sunday School classes combined."*

Another time, someone approached me after attending a class on grace I was teaching at her church. She said, "*I have been in churches for years. I have been teaching Bible classes for years. I have daily read my Bible, had my quiet times, and prayed. I have consistently practiced all the spiritual disciplines. However, I have lived in guilt all this time because I never felt I could do enough, but your class on grace changed my life!*"

That is what grace does. It powerfully changes people's lives the moment they hear it and understand it in all its truth. Romans 1:17 says, "*I am not ashamed of the gospel* [the good news about God's grace] *for it is the power of God for salvation for those who believe.*" When people hear and understand the truth of grace, combining it with belief, it totally changes their lives. Grace is the power of God that changes people's lives!

The Churches In Galatia
What Happened To All Your Joy?

One group of people who experienced the life-changing power of grace lived in the cities of the province of Galatia. When Paul visited these people, he explained to them the good news of grace. Upon learning this good news, the story of God's grace intersected with the story of their lives and produced great joy.

Because of the time he spent there, Paul started several churches on the foundation of grace. But soon after he left, the Pharisees and other religious leaders rushed to the churches in Galatia, telling them Paul was wrong, and the Law of Moses must be obeyed to become righteous before God. After hearing this, Paul sent a letter to the Galatian people. In the Bible, this letter is known as Galatians.

In this letter, Paul asks the people what happened to all their joy (Galatians 4:15). They previously welcomed Paul as if he were an angel of God or Christ himself (Galatians 4:13-14). But now they were turning away from Paul's teaching of grace and were embracing the teaching of the Pharisees and other religious leaders (Galatians 1:6-7).

Trying To Be Justified By Law

Where once Paul taught them being justified, or declared completely righteous and accepted by God, came by grace through faith, the Pharisees and religious leaders taught them being justified came by obedience to the Law of Moses. Paul told them that seeking to be justified by the Law of Moses was to actually fall away from Jesus, or fall from grace. He said in Galatians 5:4, *"Those who are trying to be justified by law have alienated themselves from Christ, they have fallen from grace."* He told them if righteousness came by the law, *"then Christ died for nothing"* (Galatians 2:21).

According to the revelation of grace given to Paul by Jesus, righteousness only comes by grace through faith. To set aside grace as the means of righteousness in favor of the law as the means to righteousness is to fall from grace and to treat the death of Jesus as nothing (Galatians 2:21).

Fallen From Grace

As a Christian, I always thought I understood the phrase *fallen from grace* until I read the phrase *fallen from grace* in the Bible. I was always taught by Bible teachers and preachers that to fall from grace was to fall back into a life of sin as a believer, meaning a life of immorality and disobedience to God. But when I was studying Paul's letter to the Galatian churches, I discovered what the phrase *fallen from grace* actually means within the context of Paul's letter to the Galatians.

In context, to fall from grace means to seek to become justified, or righteous before God, by trying to obey the Law of Moses. I summarize the meaning of the phrase *fallen from grace* in this way:

> *To fall from grace is to seek to make oneself righteous, or acceptable to God, through morality and religious activity. It is seeking to be right with God by trying not to sin and by working hard to be obedient to God rather than resting completely by faith in what Jesus freely did for us through his death and resurrection.*

Confusion About Law And Grace

This is exactly what the Pharisees did during Jesus' time. They believed righteousness was achieved through religious and moral behavior rather than received by grace through faith. These Pharisees and teachers of the law were now infiltrating the Galatian churches. They were teaching righteousness is achieved through religious activity and morality.

Consequently, the Galatian people who previously experienced the joy of grace became very confused (Galatians 1:7; 5:10). Their confusion centered on these three questions: *Is acceptance with God achieved through religious activity and morality? Is acceptance with God received by grace through faith? Or does acceptance with God come through a combination of religious activity, morality, grace, and faith?*

This is a subject I will address in the next chapter. For now, let's take a final look at how the story of God's grace impacted the story of Paul's life.

Paul, My Grace Is Sufficient For You

Remember, we first met Paul as Saul, giving his approval of the stoning of Stephen, then, angrily and violently, imprisoning many men and women, while continuing to give approval for the death of some. After his encounter with grace, his life totally changed. However, I am sure he had vivid and horrifying memories of Stephen being pounded with stone after stone, dying an excruciating death. I am sure he had guilt-ridden memories of fathers and mothers being dragged away from their towns with their children crying out in horror.

Haunted By Past Memories

More than likely, whenever he saw children, he was reminded of his past. Surely, the memories of his past haunted him, possibly tormenting him day and night. Shame, guilt, condemnation, and regret weighed heavily upon him.

We can't forget, Paul was human, just like us, capable of doing terrible things and feeling tremendous emotional pain. I believe it was these tormenting memories, coupled with shame, guilt, condemnation, and regret, that Paul referred to as his thorn in the flesh (2 Corinthians 12:7).

Paul said his thorn in the flesh was a messenger from Satan sent to torment him I believe the mission of this satanic messenger was to attack Paul through the memories of his past, tormenting him with shame, guilt, condemnation, and regret, much the same way Satan attacks us through the memories of our past. Tormented by these memories and weighed down by shame, guilt, condemnation, and regrets, Paul cried out to Jesus three times to take these tormenting memories and feelings of shame, guilt, condemnation, and regret away, but Jesus responded to Paul by saying, *"My grace is sufficient for you, for my power is made perfect in weakness"* (2 Corinthians 12:8).

Healed By Grace

Essentially, Jesus was telling Paul his unconditional love, unearned blessings, unmerited kindness, and unlimited forgiveness were what he needed to find healing from the memories haunting him and to find relief from the shame, guilt, condemnation, and regrets weighing heavily upon him. Rather than dwelling on his past, Jesus told Paul to dwell on his grace. By dwelling on grace, healing and relief would come.

Toward the end of Paul's life, while sharing the good news of God's grace as the way to enter the kingdom of God, he quoted a verse from Isaiah which said God would bring healing to the hearts of people if they would turn to him (Acts 28:23-27). God's heart is a heart of grace that wants to heal those who are haunted by their memories and release those feeling the weight of their shame, guilt, condemnation, and regrets.

Are You Tormented By Your Memories?

So many people live daily tormented by the memories of something wrong they did. You may be one of these people. If you are tormented by your memories and weighed down by shame, guilt, condemnation, and regret, hear Jesus telling you what he told Paul:

"My grace is sufficient for you, for my power is made perfect in your weakness. Receive my grace. Receive my unconditional love, unearned blessings, unmerited kindness, and unlimited forgiveness. I love you. I accept you. I have forgiven you."

8

The Story Of Law And Grace

As we learned in the last chapter, the people of Galatia were very confused regarding how a person becomes righteous, or accepted by God. Initially, they experienced joy because they learned from Paul that righteousness is received by grace through faith in Jesus. But eventually, some religious leaders infiltrated their churches telling them righteousness is achieved through religious activity and morality. Others told them righteousness was achieved through a combination of religious activity, morality, and faith in Jesus. You can imagine their confusion.

Their confusion centered on these three questions: *Is acceptance with God achieved through religious activity and morality? Is acceptance with God received by grace through faith? Or does acceptance with God come through a combination of religious activity, morality, grace, and faith?*

How Is A Person Accepted By God?
Unfortunately, the confusion of the people within the Galatian churches is the same confusion existing in the minds of many people in churches today. Day after day they wonder if they have done enough good works to gain God's acceptance. Have they prayed enough, witnessed enough, read the Bible enough, memorized enough verses, gone to church enough, fasted enough, served enough, or given enough? Some live confidently believing they have, while others live fearing they haven't.

Some believe acceptance with God comes through faith alone, while others believe acceptance with God is a combination of faith plus works such as meeting religious or church expectations, having spiritual experiences, or following moral standards. Still others are very confused, not knowing which of these it takes to be accepted by God.

The best place to discover what it takes to be accepted by God is the Bible. What does the Bible say? Is righteousness gained through obedience to the law or a commitment to a religious system and moral standard? Is righteousness received by grace through faith or is righteousness achieved by a mixture of law, grace, and faith? Must a person meet specific expectations or have spiritual experiences to gain God's acceptance? In the Bible, the book of Romans provides the answer to these questions.

All Are Unrighteous

In Romans chapters one and two, we learn all people are unrighteous. Both the nonreligious and religious and the immoral and moral are unrighteous. In Romans chapter three, we discover everyone is alike because all have sinned. We are all immoral and unrighteous before God. There is not one person who has ever lived, other than Jesus, who is a moral, righteous person...not even one (Romans 3:9-10)!

All Are Guilty

Romans 3:19-20 says everyone is guilty of breaking the law, meaning the Ten Commandments. The Jewish people had the Ten Commandments written on stone by God and given to them through Moses (Romans 2:12, 13, 17). They had all sinned and broken the commandments. All other people, referred to as Gentiles, had the requirements of the Ten Commandments written on their hearts (Romans 2:14-15). They, too, had sinned and broken the commandments.

So, we learn in Romans that everyone in the world has broken the Ten Commandments and is accountable to God (Romans 3:19-20). We are all guilty before God. We are all silent before God. We are all sinful before God (Romans 3:23). God has seen every thought we have had and every deed we have done. He knows our private thoughts and desires (Romans 2:16). He knows our public deeds. There is nothing we can say.

Because we have all broken the Ten Commandments, no one will be declared righteous in God's sight by obeying them (Romans 3:20). No one can gain God's acceptance by following them.

The Ten Commandments are God's moral standards. We know lying is wrong. We know stealing is wrong. We know adultery is wrong. We know coveting is wrong. We know putting something before God is wrong. We read it in the Ten Commandments. We feel it in our hearts. And, if we are honest, all of us would agree with God by admitting we have all done wrong. We have all broken the Ten Commandments. We have all sinned (Romans 3:23).

The Ten Commandments Show Us How Sinful We Are

The good news is God never gave us the Ten Commandments, the law, so if we obeyed it, he would declare us righteous before him. He gave us the commandments to show us how sinful we are, so we would receive his grace by placing our faith in Jesus (Romans 3:19-25; Galatians 3:21). The Ten Commandments are God's way of revealing to us our sin, so he can release to us his grace.

The Ten Commandments Show Us Our Need For Grace

Romans 5:20 says, *"The law was added so that the trespass* [sin] *may increase."* The purpose of the law was to increase the sins of people, so we would see our sin and need for grace and so the story of God's grace would intersect with the story of our lives.

The second part of Romans 5:20 says, *"But where sin increased, grace increased all the more."* It is when the story of God's grace intersects with the story of our lives that we can really begin to live. Romans 5:17 and 21 says it is by receiving God's abundant provision of grace for our sin that we will reign in life, or really begin to live!

A law can never impart life (Galatians 3:21), only grace can. A law can never bring a person who is spiritually dead to life. Only God's unconditional love, unearned blessings, unmerited kindness, and unlimited forgiveness to us through Jesus bring us life.

We Become Righteous By Believing

We become righteous before God by receiving his grace. We receive God's grace by believing. According to Romans 3:22-25, righteousness is given freely to those who believe, to those who have faith in Jesus' payment for their sins. These verses say, *"This righteousness from God comes through faith in Jesus Christ to all who believe...and are justified freely by his grace through the redemption that came by Jesus Christ."*

Righteousness is not earned through a commitment to a religious system or obedience to moral standards, such as the Ten Commandments. It is not earned by meeting the expectations of your church or having spiritual experiences. It is not earned by practicing a set of spiritual disciplines such as reading the Bible, praying, having a quiet time, memorizing verses, fasting, or going to church. Righteousness is freely given to us by faith in Jesus alone.

Romans 3:28 says, *"For we maintain, a person is justified by faith apart from observing the law."* Romans 4:1-8 says, *"However, to the man who does not work but trusts God who justifies the wicked, his faith is credited as righteousness."*

What Must I Do?

One rich man who thought righteousness was achieved through obedience to the Ten Commandments asked Jesus what he needed to do to gain eternal life, meaning to live eternally in the kingdom of God (Luke 18:18-27). Jesus, knowing his heart, told him to keep the commandments of God. The man replied he kept the commandments since he was a child. Then Jesus told him to go sell all he had, give to the poor, and follow him, and he would have eternal life. His disciples asked him how anyone could gain eternal life if this man could not, since this man had obeyed the law from childhood, or so he thought. Jesus replied, *"What is impossible with men is possible with God"* (Luke 18:27).

It is impossible for us to save ourselves. We can only be saved by grace through faith. This was the point Jesus was making. The man believed he could save himself through obedience to the Ten Commandments. So Jesus held the Ten Commandments in front of him as a mirror to show him his sinful heart. Jesus showed him, through the law, he had not obeyed the law since childhood but had broken the commandments by putting money above God, which is idolatry, and loving money more than people.

Rather than walking away sad, if the man would have cried out to Jesus, *"Have mercy upon me, a sinner"*, he would have walked away justified, or righteous before God. Yet the man had no concept of his sin. Instead, just like the Pharisees, he boasted in his religious activity and his morality, having no awareness of his unrighteousness and need for grace (Luke 18:18-27). This man had so much pride that even Jesus and his use of Ten Commandments could not convince him he was a sinner in need of grace.

God's Promise To Make Us Righteous By Grace

In chapter two, we learned God made a promise to Abraham. This promise was God would bless the people of the world through Abraham. It was a promise of grace through which God would justify, or declare people to be righteous before him through faith in Jesus (Galatians 3:6-18).

Grace is everything God has done for us through Jesus to make us righteous. Faith is accepting what he has done. Romans 5:1-2 says, *"Therefore, since we have been justified* [declared by God to be righteous before him] *through faith, we have peace with God* [no longer under judgment for our sins], *through whom we have gained access by faith into this grace we now stand."*

Think about it. Would you rather seek eternal life, or entrance into God's eternal kingdom, through your own commitment to a religious system, obedience to the Ten Commandments, or by standing in God's grace? Would you rather seek acceptance with God by faithfully practicing spiritual disciplines or by standing in God's grace? Definitely standing in God's grace. This is because a commitment to a religious system, obedience to the Ten Commandments, or practicing a set of spiritual disciplines will never achieve righteousness. They will never result in acceptance with God. They will never qualify us for entrance into God's kingdom.

Righteousness is required to enter God's kingdom. We can't earn it. It is impossible. God freely gives it to us by grace, and we simply receive it by faith. Now that is good news!

Something else to think about. If being righteous could be gained through a commitment to a religious system or obedience to the Ten Commandments, then why did Jesus die? If acceptance with God could be earned by practicing a set of religious disciplines, then why did Jesus die? He died because none of these remove the penalty of sin. No matter how religious or moral people may think they are, or appear to be, and no matter how much people practice a set of spiritual disciplines, they are still under the penalty of sin. Only grace removes us from the penalty of sin and makes us right with God. Galatians 2:21 says, *"Therefore, I do not set aside grace, for If righteousness could be gained through the law, then Christ died for nothing!"*

We are encouraged in the Bible to stand in grace and not to set aside grace. This means for us not to step away from grace or put away grace to follow a religious system, moral standard, or set of spiritual disciplines to gain God's acceptance.

The Bible speaks about not allowing people to put you under their religious system, moral standard, or set of spiritual disciplines to earn God's acceptance (Galatians 3:1; 4:17; 5:1; 7-10; Colossians 2:13-23). Religious systems, moral standards, and spiritual disciplines are weak and useless ways to become righteous before God (Galatians 4:9-10). Only by grace through faith do we become righteous before God.

For several years, I allowed people to put me under a set of spiritual disciplines. They convinced me that if I consistently prayed, read my Bible, had daily quiet times, memorized verses, and daily confessed my sins, then I would grow spiritually and stay right with

God. I would feel good if I practiced these disciplines but guilty if I did not. This left me in a constant state of confusion about where I stood with God. It left me frustrated. You may have had this same experience.

Trying To Become Righteous Through The Law
Frustrated With Ourselves

Romans 7:14-25 describes one man who had a frustrating experience seeking to become righteous before God by adhering to a religious system and following a moral standard. However, the more he attempted to adhere to a religious system and follow a moral standard, the more aware of his sin and frustrated he became.

This person's religious system and moral standard was the Ten Commandments. He described himself as living as a slave to the commandments. Every day he chained himself to the commandments, seeking to obey them, hoping to become righteous and gain God's acceptance through his obedience. What this person discovered, in seeking to become righteous before God through obedience to the Ten Commandments, was the very commandment he was trying to obey brought more sin into his life, ultimately resulting in death (Romans 7:8-11).

As we have learned, increasing sin was God's purpose for the Ten Commandments (Romans 5:20; 7:13). This man became chained to guilt, shame, and condemnation because, rather than obeying the commandments, he sinned even more. The law established a standard of moral behavior for him, educated him about sin, exposed his sinful heart, and then sentenced him to be executed for his disobedience.

In his process of seeking to become righteous before God through obedience to the Ten Commandments, he became frustrated with himself. He discovered that adhering to a religious system or following a moral standard to become righteous before God was impossible. Even though the Ten Commandments were good, they showed him how sinful he was, much like an x-ray machine shows someone his sickness. They only problem is the x-ray machine can't cure the sickness. The law shows us we are sinful but can't cure our sinfulness. The law showed him his sin but had no cure. So he found himself in a terrible condition, asking a very good question: *"Who will rescue me from this body of death?"* (Romans 7:25).

Who Will Rescue Me?

This is a good question. Maybe you have discovered what this person discovered, that no matter how sincere you are and how hard you try to achieve righteousness, or acceptance with God, by adhering to a religious system, following a moral standard, or practicing a set of spiritual disciplines, you keep falling short. You keep feeling guilty. You feel you are letting God down. You feel like you are a disappointment to God.

You know yourself. You know your thoughts. You know your desires. You know your deeds. You know your sin. And you know God knows. Like this person, you have become frustrated with yourself for not measuring up. You feel rejection from the very God with whom you are seeking to find acceptance. So, you ask yourself the same question as this man: *"Who will rescue me from this body of death?"* His answer...your answer...the answer..."*Thanks be to God - through Jesus Christ our Lord!*" (Romans 7:25).

God, Thank You For Grace!

This part of the Bible was originally written in Greek. The word *thanks* in this verse is *charis*, the Greek word for grace. Here is what I think the man is saying in this verse, *"God, thank you so much for the grace you have provided for me through Jesus that rescues me from the condemnation of sin!"* The only way we can be rescued from the condemnation of sin is grace. And for his grace, we say *"Thank you!"*

God, with whom we seek acceptance, provides the solution to the condemnation for our sin. The solution is grace. He sent Jesus to take the condemnation for our sins (Romans 8:3). That is why the Bible says in Romans 8:1 *"there is now no condemnation for those who are in Christ Jesus."* Why is there no condemnation for those who have come to faith in Jesus? Because Jesus took all our condemnation upon himself through his death. As a result, there is no condemnation for those who have faith in Jesus.

So, we see the law, the Ten Commandments, served its purpose in this person's life. It showed him his sin and need for God's grace. Since the law completed its work in this man, convincing him of his sinfulness and bringing him to faith in Jesus as the way to become accepted by God, he was no longer in need of the law. The law did its job. As a result, he was not under law. He was now under grace.

If you have come to faith in Jesus, you are not under the law either. You are under grace. As a result, you do not have to try to gain God's acceptance by adhering to a religious system, following a moral standard, or practicing a set of spiritual disciplines. You are accepted by God because you have placed your faith in Jesus. God has declared you righteous. On your good days you are righteous. On your not so good days you are righteous. This is because righteousness is given to you as a gift of grace. It is free. It can't be earned. It can't be removed. It can only be received by faith.

Not Under Law But Under Grace

Romans 6:14 says those who have come to faith in Jesus are not under law, the Ten Commandments, but under grace. We have now been declared righteous by God and relate to him by grace not law.

Are You Saying We Can Sin More?

This understanding of grace always leads to a couple of questions. They are the same questions Paul was asked many times when he taught about law and grace (Romans 6:1, 15). They are the same questions I am asked constantly when I teach on law and grace. Here are the questions: *"Are you saying we can sin all we want because the more we sin the more grace we get? Are you saying we can sin now that we are not under law but under grace?"*

The truth is unless these questions are asked of those claiming to preach the gospel, such as pastors and Bible teachers, they are not truly preaching the gospel. These questions posed to the ones truly proclaiming the gospel are evidence they are really communicating the good news about all God has done for us through the life, death, and resurrection of Jesus. If these questions cannot be asked of those claiming to preach the gospel, then they are not proclaiming the gospel.

Charles Swindoll in his book, *Grace Awakening*, shares the following insight about a person proclaiming to preach the gospel, yet who cannot be falsely accused of giving someone a license to sin:

> *I can assure you of this: Grace-killing ministers will never have that charge brought against them* (page 41).

Dr. Swindoll also quotes Dr. Martin Lloyd Jones about the same subject:

The true preaching of the gospel of salvation by grace alone always leads to the possibility of this charge [giving people a license to sin] *being brought against it. There is no better test as to whether a man is teaching the New Testament gospel of salvation than this, that some people might misunderstand it and misinterpret to mean that it really amounts to this, that because you are saved by grace alone it does not matter at all what you do; you can go on sinning as much as you like...That is a very good test of gospel preaching. If my preaching and presentation of the gospel does not expose it to that misunderstanding, then it is not the gospel...that is exactly what the Church of Rome said about the preaching of Martin Luther...It was also brought against George Whitefield two hundred years ago...I would say to all preachers: If your preaching of salvation has not been misunderstood* [as being light on sin and giving people a license to sin]*, then you had better examine your sermons again, and you had better make sure that you are really preaching the salvation that is offered in the New Testament to the ungodly, to the sinner, to those who are dead in trespasses and sins, to those who are enemies of God. There is this kind of dangerous element about the true presentation of the doctrine of salvation* (pages 39-40).

We Can't Be Afraid To Teach Grace

Those who teach the biblical truths of grace will be accused by many people of being light on sin and giving people a license to sin. These accusations were not only made against Paul but were also made against Jesus by the Pharisees. As teachers of grace, we can never let the fear of the "modern day Pharisees" keep us from proclaiming the fullness of grace.

Once I was having a conversation with a fellow pastor, he told me this: *"Brad, I would love to teach the message of grace like you do in your church, because what you are teaching is biblical. But if I did, I would lose my church and my job."* Sadly, this pastor's teaching was designed to please some of the people in his church rather than Jesus.

Paul spoke about this desire to please people with what one teaches rather than seeking to please God with the teaching of grace:

"Am I trying to win the approval of men, or of God [with what I teach]? Or am I trying to please men? If I were still trying to please men, I would not be a servant of Christ."

Galatians 1:10-11

Paul used very strong language for those claiming to preach the gospel, yet who did not fully communicate the message of grace. They led people to believe they must adhere to a religious system or follow a moral standard for acceptance with God. In writing to the churches in Galatia, he said:

I am amazed that you are so quickly deserting Him who called you by the grace of Christ [the good news of grace when Jesus paid your sin penalty in full through his death, and by faith in Jesus you are righteous], *for a different gospel* [adhering to a religious system or following a moral standard for righteousness]; *which is really not another; only there are some who are disturbing you and want to distort the gospel of Christ. But even if we, or an angel from heaven, should preach to you a gospel contrary to what we have preached to you* [righteousness is through grace and received by faith]*, he is to be accursed! As we have said before, so I say again now, if any man is preaching to you a gospel contrary to what you received, he is to be accursed!*

Galatians 1:6-9 (New American Standard Bible)

These are extremely strong words from the very one to whom the ascended Jesus revealed the message of grace (Galatians 1:11-12).

It Can't Be Done! I Can't Be Saved!

Once someone approach me saying, *"It can't be done! I can't be saved!"* I asked, *"Why not?"* He responded, *"I can't live up to what I am being told. I know me. I know my heart. I know my sins. I know my weaknesses. I can't do it!"* He was told if he puts his hand to the plow and looks back he cannot be saved. He was told he must deny himself, pick up his cross, and daily follow Jesus if he wants to be saved. He was told he must love God with all his heart, soul, mind, and strength, and to love others as himself if he wants to be saved.

These are the words of Jesus. However, the reason for Jesus' words was to convince those who thought salvation was through one's commitment, faithfulness, obedience, and love they needed grace. Jesus was telling them the commitment, faithfulness, obedience, and love needed for salvation was required every day with all of their heart, soul, mind, and strength for the rest of their lives. They could never look back. They could never put their cross down...not even once! Everything they did must be motivated by complete love for God and others. They could in no way, not ever, act selfishly.

Who can do this? Who can every day for the rest of his life take up his cross and never look back? Who can love God and others with all his heart, soul, mind, and strength? Who can love others as he loves himself? No one. The only one who ever took up his cross daily and never looked back was Jesus. The only one who has ever loved God with all his heart, soul, mind, and strength, and others as himself was Jesus. The only one who never acted selfishly but served others in love was Jesus. His ultimate act of love was serving us by offering himself for our sins through his death.

We are saved by his love for us not our love for God or others. We are saved by grace through faith in Jesus, the one who never looked back, who took up his cross daily, and died for our sins. If our love was good enough, then we do not need his love. If our cross was good enough, then we do not need his cross. We would then have something to boast about. Yet we have nothing to boast about. We can't boast about our commitment. We can't boast about our faithfulness. We can't boast about our love. We all fall short because of sin. We can only boast about Jesus and the cross he took up for us by grace, so we could be freely given righteousness, enabling us to possess eternal life in his kingdom (1 Corinthians 1:30-31; Galatians 6:14; Ephesians 2:8-9).

Back To The Question: Can We Sin More?

So, this takes us back to the questions originally asked: *If salvation is all of Jesus and none of us...if salvation requires no obedience on our part, but is given to us freely by grace through faith...if we are no longer under law, but under grace, then can we use grace as a license to sin? Can we sin more so we receive more grace? Can we sin even more now that we are not under law but under grace?*

So, what is the answer to these questions? Paul answered these questions in Romans 6. His answer was: *Absolutely not! Don't even think that way!* He asks how anyone can live in sin, meaning rebellion to God, when the very reason this person came to Jesus was to receive forgiveness of sins and begin a relationship with God.

An illustration I like to use in teaching through Romans 6 is this: Coming to faith in Jesus and then using his grace as a license to sin would be like someone getting married then asking, *"Now that I am married, can I live as single person since how I live will have no effect on whether or not I am married?"*

We Have A New Life

When two people get married they are identifying themselves with one another. They become one flesh...man and woman become husband and wife. They are in a relationship now. Their old identities are gone. They have a whole new life together as a married couple. They didn't marry each other so they could live independently from one another and commit adultery against each other. They married each other to enjoy a love relationship.

We Are In A Relationship With God

In the same way, Paul, in Romans 6, tells us that when we identified ourselves with Jesus Christ through receiving his grace by faith, it was for the purpose of beginning a new life. We did not receive his grace so we could continue to sin. We received his grace so we could enter into a relationship with God. We are to consider ourselves dead to sin, no longer living in willful rebellion to God by living an immoral lifestyle but having begun a relationship with him and allowing him to change our lives.

This does not mean we will not be tempted to sin, struggle with sin, or even be addicted to a sin. There will be conflict between the Spirit of Christ in us and the flesh (Galatians 5:16-17). The flesh is the sinful thoughts and desires within all of us (Ephesians 2:3). However, since we are not under law but under grace, we do not say we can give ourselves over to these thoughts and desires. Instead, we offer ourselves to God as instruments of righteousness rather than offering ourselves to sin. By offering ourselves to God as instruments of righteousness, we are giving ourselves to him for his beautiful song of grace to be played in our lives. If we offer ourselves to sin, we are giving ourselves to sin for its destructive song of pain and heartache to be played in our lives.

Paul tells us in Romans 6 that the purpose of grace is to set us free from sin's destruction, not to set us free to sin. He says sin will not be our master because we are not under law but under grace. Grace brings us into a love relationship with God as our loving Father while law keeps us under his condemnation as judge. If we view God as a judge, whose law we must obey, or as a god who will curse and condemn us for sin, sin will remain in control of our lives. This is because, out of fear of God's punishment and condemnation, we will live preoccupied with not sinning. Whatever we are preoccupied with will control us.

Living Under The Law Of Dad

In baseball, if a child lives in fear of missing a ground ball, striking out, or dropping a fly ball, he will live up to his fears. Many children live in this fearful environment at all their games. They live under "dad's law" of not striking out, missing a ground ball, or dropping a fly ball. If they do, the condemnation, anger, and rejection of dad will come upon them.

These children crave their dad's acceptance but live in fear of his rejection. So, what do they do? They try hard not to make an error. Yet the harder they try, the more errors they make. This is because they are playing fearfully under "dad's law". Law produces failure. With each error, the glaring look of disapproval comes upon them from dad.

The child who plays in grace has a much different experience because he is convinced of his dad's love, acceptance, and kindness. He knows that no matter how many errors he makes, he is loved and accepted by his dad, and his dad will be full of kindness to him. As a result, he will make less errors because he is not concentrating on failing but is focused on enjoying the game, knowing, success or failure, he is loved and accepted by his dad!

Some children who play under the "law of dad" rather than the "grace of dad" eventually leave the sport altogether because they are weary from playing under so much fear and pressure. This is what happens to some Christians who are living under law rather than grace. They crave God's love and kindness but live in fear of his anger and rejection. They are trying not to strike out spiritually. They are trying not to miss a spiritual ground ball. They are trying not to drop a spiritual fly ball. Yet, glancing up into the bleachers of heaven, they sense the disapproving eyes of God glaring down upon them. They live in fear his anger will come upon them if they make an error. So they quit. They give up.

Some who began a relationship with God through faith in Jesus have given up and quit on their relationship with God. The reason why is they were living under law and not grace. They were living in fear of God's punishment and condemnation, his anger and rejection. They continued to struggle with sin, as we all do, but no one ever taught them the fullness of grace. So what did they do? They gave up. They quit. They went back into their lives of sin, convinced they were under God's judgment, convinced they had "fallen from grace".

They were not using grace as a license to sin. But like all of us, they were battling with the conflict between their flesh and the Spirit of Jesus in them (Galatians 5:16-18). Had they been taught and understood the truths of grace, they would never have quit on their relationship with God, and sin would not have taken such control of their lives.

Others, living in fear under law, hide their sins and struggles, secretly making promises to God they will do better, but they continue to fail over and over. Consequently, they live believing God is disappointed with them and has rejected them.

Law keeps God as judge over our lives where we constantly live in fear of his anger, rejection, and condemnation. Grace ushers us into a love relationship with God where we are assured of his love, kindness, acceptance, and forgiveness. This assurance enables us to be transparent with him in an open, honest relationship, with no fear of his anger or rejection. In this love relationship, we call God our loving Father. This is called the Spirit-filled life.

9

The Story Of The Spirit-Filled Life

To understand the Spirit-filled life, we must have a proper understanding of law and grace. In the previous chapter, we discovered we are no longer under law but under grace. This means we no longer relate to God as judge, living in fear of his anger, rejection, and condemnation. We now relate to God as our Father, assured of his love, kindness, acceptance, and forgiveness. This is the story of the Spirit-filled life.

God Sent The Spirit of Jesus To Live In Us

Galatians 4:4-7 says, *"But when the time had fully come, God sent his Son, born of a woman, born under law, to redeem those under law, that we might receive the full rights of sons. Because you are sons, God sent the Spirit of his Son into our hearts, the Spirit who cries out, "Abba, Father". So you are no longer a slave, but a son; and since you are a son, God has made you an heir."*

In God's perfect timing, he sent Jesus to fulfill the law, which are the Ten Commandments. Jesus fulfilled the law by living a life of perfect love, both inwardly and outwardly. He is the only one who ever loved God with all his heart, soul, mind, and strength, and loved others as himself. By fulfilling the law, he became qualified to pay our sin penalty. After Jesus fulfilled the law on our behalf and paid our sin penalty through his death, God set us free from the law and sent the Spirit of Jesus to live in our hearts (Romans 7:6; Galatians 4:4-6).

The Spirit Cries Out "Abba, Father"

The Spirit of Jesus in us cries out to God, *"Abba, Father"* (Galatians 4:6). The word *"Abba"* is the word Jewish boys and girls used in Jesus' time to refer to their dads. In America, we say *"daddy"*. Abba is a word that has love bursting forth from it. It is a word describing the joy, peace, patience, kindness, goodness, gentleness, and faithfulness of a daddy toward a child. It has no hint of fear or rejection in it. None at all!

This is the kind of relationship we have with God under grace. It is a relationship where we experience the love, joy, peace, patience, kindness, goodness, and faithfulness of God as our Father. On our good days and bad days, God is a Father who consistently responds to us in love. Because of his love, we do not have to live in fear of his rejection or punishment (1 John 4:18) but are guaranteed of his acceptance.

Romans 8:15 says, *"For you did not receive a spirit that makes you a slave again to fear, but you received the Spirit of sonship. And by him we cry, "Abba, Father." The Spirit himself testifies with our spirit that we are God's children."* The Bible says we are *"God's dearly loved children"* (Ephesians 5:1). He has great love for us (1 John 3:1). We are his dearly and greatly loved children!

We Do Not Have To Live In Fear

God did not give us a spirit of fear when it comes to our relationship with him, but one of love. Because we have a Father in God who loves as he does, we do not have to live in fear of God's wrath and punishment like a slave. A slave lives every day in fear of his owner's punishment. He has no relationship with his owner. To his owner, the slave is nothing more than a piece of property, existing only to perform tasks. The owner demands those tasks be performed. And when those tasks are not performed up to his standards, he punishes his slave. So, every day, the slave lives in fear of his owner's wrath and punishment.

The Bible says God is nothing like this. He is not an abusive slave owner who demands we perform, and if we don't, he sends his wrath upon us. According to Galatians 4:8, this slave-owner image of God is a false god. This verse says, *"Formerly, when you did not know God, you were slaves to those who by nature are not gods."* The slave-owner god is a false god created by religion. It is a false god people create that demands we live up to his standards, and if not, we are punished. It is a false god who has no love for us, only expectations. Grace sets us free by releasing us from the enslavement of this false god that only exists in our minds.

This false god is not the God who created the world and then stepped down into the world he created to bring us grace, so he could be in a love relationship with us (2 Corinthians 5:18-6:2). The God who created the world is the God who was the Word who became flesh. He is the God full of grace and truth, blessing us with grace after grace after grace (John 1:16-17). He lived among us, eventually died for us, then rose from the dead. The God who created the world is the one who loves the world so much that he sent his One and Only Son into the world, not to condemn the world, but so the people of the world who believed would enter his eternal kingdom of love, peace, joy, gladness, healing, and righteousness (John 3:16-17). He is the God who sent the Spirit of Jesus to live in our hearts, enabling us to call him *"Abba, Father."*

God Loves You And Wants To be In A Relationship With You
The true God is the God who loves you and desires to be in a relationship with you. For you to be in this relationship with him, he

had to pay your sin penalty. His law was given to convince you of your sin. Once you see your sin, you realize you need his grace. By realizing your need for grace, you turn to him by placing your faith in Jesus. After trusting in Jesus, God releases you from the law and sends the Spirit of Jesus into your heart, enabling you to know to him as *"Abba, Father"*.

Turning Away From A Relationship And Back To Rules
The people in Galatia initially understood this truth. They were free from the law and were enjoying a relationship with God as their loving Father. But when the religious leaders surfaced in Galatia, they did not stand their ground in grace. Instead, they allowed religious leaders to place them back under religious rules, requirements, and rituals to gain acceptance with God (Galatians 3:3). They were turning away from God's grace by turning back to a religious and moral system to find acceptance with God (Galatians 1:6). In doing so, they were becoming enslaved again to the very religious system they once escaped through grace.

Galatians 4:9 says, *"...how is it that you are turning back to those weak and miserable principles? Do you wish to be enslaved to them all over again?"* Where they were once enjoying a love relationship with God as their Father through the Spirit of Jesus, they returned to living in fear of his condemnation as their judge under law. To release themselves from this fear, they were seeking through a religious system to appease an angry god that did not exist. Consequently, their joy disappeared and was replaced by misery (Galatians 4:15).

Two Rules Religious People Live By

Rule #1: Seek God's Forgiveness Daily

Many are taught by those overseeing their religious system, church, or ministry to live by the rule of seeking God's forgiveness daily. Rather than being taught all their sins have been completely forgiven and that forgiveness is received through faith in Jesus, they are taught they need to continually ask God for forgiveness each day. Initially, they are excited about coming to faith in Jesus. Then spiritual leaders tell them they must follow the daily religious rule of seeking God's forgiveness to maintain acceptance and stay in fellowship with God (close to God). This is what happened to me.

I was told if I wanted to maintain acceptance and fellowship with God, I needed to daily ask God to forgive me. I was told I needed to make sure I had no "unconfessed sins" in my life. I had become enslaved, trying to adhere to a religious system and follow religious rules imposed upon me by others. I was certainly not enjoying my relationship with God. Joy disappeared from my heart and was replaced with misery as I sought to daily ask God for forgiveness rather than accept and enjoy the forgiveness freely given to me by God (Ephesians 1:6-8).

Rule #2: Stay in Fellowship with God Consistently

Others are told they need to repent daily, immediately confessing their sins, so they can be forgiven and stay in fellowship with God. By fellowship with God, they mean experiencing closeness with God and staying in right relationship him. They are told if they have unconfessed sins in their lives they will be out of fellowship with God, and God will not hear their prayers or bless their lives. Some are told, if they have unconfessed sin in their lives and die, they will go straight to hell. So, they live hoping they have confessed every sin but fearing they haven't. We will take a deeper look at this in the next chapter.

Maybe you were told in the religious system, organization, church, or denomination you are a part of that you must do something to obtain or maintain salvation, acceptance, forgiveness, or fellowship with God. So rather than concentrating on enjoying your relationship with God through all that he did for you in Jesus, you have become enslaved to the daily, weekly, and yearly requirements imposed on you by your spiritual leaders. Some days you feel good about your relationship with God because you have done well following these requirements, and other days you feel bad because you have not done so well. I have good news for you. The same good news enabling me to escape from religious slavery will enable you to escape, too!

Good News! You Do Not Have To Earn What God Has Freely Given

Here is the good news. Jesus, through grace, did everything for you to bring you close to God and into a relationship with him. You do not have to obtain or maintain salvation, acceptance, forgiveness, or fellowship with God by adhering to the rules and requirements imposed on you. Through grace, these have been freely provided for you in Jesus. You do not have to earn what God has freely given (Romans 3:23; 1 Corinthians 2:12; Ephesians 1:6). Just receive his grace by faith in Jesus, and once you have done this, you can enjoy a close relationship with God as your loving Father!

We Died To Religious Systems

Romans 7:6 says, *"But now, by dying to what once bound us* [the law - a religious system]*, we have been released from the law so that we* *serve* [relate to God] *in the new way of the Spirit* [grace]*, and not in the old way of the written code* [law]*.”*

We died to the law when we received God's grace through faith in Jesus. We then became alive to God through the Spirit of Jesus inside of us, calling God our loving Father.

God Doesn't Want Us Living By A Law

God's plan has always been to release us from the law and send his Spirit into our hearts. His plan was not for us to live in obedience to his law, or any requirements or rules, but to experience his love, and then live a life of love produced within our hearts by his Spirit. By living a life of love, we would not need a law. Deuteronomy 30:6 says, *“The Lord your God will circumcise your hearts and the hearts of your descendants so that you may love him with all your heart and with all your soul and live.”* Romans 2:29 says, *“...circumcision is of the heart, by the Spirit, not by the written code.”*

God had given the law, which said to love others as we love ourselves (Leviticus 19:18) and to love him with all our heart, soul, and strength (Deuteronomy 6:5). Jesus said every other law in the Old Testament hung upon these two laws (Matthew 22:37-40). So, we see the law is based on love, but no one can obey the law. This is because sin has replaced God's love in our hearts. Had our hearts been filled with love, there would have been no need for the law.

Disobedience to his law of love is sin. Jesus, by living a life of love, fulfilled the law for us, died for our sins, rose from the dead, and now lives in us by his Spirit. The Spirit of Jesus in us enables us to experience God's love as our Father. This experience of our Father's love circumcises our hearts, or changes our hearts inwardly, so we can love God and others.

A Law Can't Change The Heart

A law can never change the heart of a person. A law controls a person's behavior through fear for a short time but can never change a person's heart for a lifetime. For example, a person who is breaking the law of his community by driving over the speed limit will slow down for a short amount of time if he thinks a police officer is just around the corner with a radar gun. What motivated him to slow down was not his love for his community and safety of others but his fear of getting a ticket. As soon as he passes the area where there was a police officer with a radar gun, he speeds back up and proceeds to drive beyond the speed limit. His driving behavior was controlled by fear for a short time, not for a lifetime.

The Law Is Based On Our Selfishness

Sometimes a law is used to control someone's behavior with both fear and reward. For example, a dad tells his son that if he is obedient, he will get an ice cream cone, but if he is disobedient, his toys will be taken away. Wanting an ice cream cone and fearing his toys will be taken away, the son obeys externally. However, his motivation for obedience was not love for his dad but for selfish reasons...getting an ice cream cone and not losing his toys. If the child was controlled inwardly by love for his dad, then his dad would not need to motivate with fear of toys being taken away or reward of an ice cream cone. The dad could simply tell his son to act in a certain way and the son would do it because he knew his dad loved him and he loved his dad. Then, having nothing to do with his behavior, his dad would take him out to the best ice cream shop in town to enjoy a cone of ice cream together!

The Book Of The Law

God put a behavior system in place much like the one just described. It was called the Book of the Covenant or the Book of the Law (Exodus 24:7; Deuteronomy 28:61), also known as the written code (Romans 2:29; 7:6).

In the Old Testament, God told the people of Israel, whose hearts were reflections of every other person's heart in the world, that if they obeyed the Book of the Covenant, he would bless them, and if they disobeyed, he would curse them. This was the only way God could motivate good behavior among the people to provide and protect them from hurting one another and destroying their nation. He wanted them to fulfill their purpose, which was being a light to the other nations of his salvation (Isaiah 49:6; Luke 2:32; Acts 13:47).

God had to appeal to their selfishness through the law, which made him their judge. However, the greatest desire of his heart was not for them to relate to him as judge but to know him as their loving Father who had nothing but good stored up for them in his heart:

> *"How gladly I would treat you like sons and give you a desirable land, the most beautiful inheritance of any nation. I thought you would call me 'Father' ..."*
>
> Jeremiah 3:19

God Longs For A Love Relationship

God's heart is that of a father who longs for a relationship with his child, but his child completely rebels to his father's love. In this rebellion, the father must become a judge, dispensing law in hopes of protecting his son from destroying his own life, so he can reach his potential. But no matter how much the father tries to draw his son back with his love, while at the same time delivering consequences for his son's rebellion, the son continues to defy his father's love, bringing destruction into his life.

The father's heart is broken because he loves his son so much. It pains the father to see his son destroying his life and to have to discipline his son, when all the father ever wanted was to bless his son and enjoy a love relationship with him.

God Draws Us With Loving Kindness

This was the heart of God toward the nation of Israel. Remember, the nation of Israel reflected the hearts of all people. God was a loving father, only wanting to give them his love and blessings. Yet, as a son rebelling to his father's love, the nation of Israel rebelled against God, putting themselves under God's judgment and condemnation. Even though God had to act as judge toward Israel by delivering punishment, he continued to draw them toward him with everlasting love and kindness, seeking only to bless them:

> *"I have loved you with an everlasting love; I have*
> *drawn you with loving-kindness."*
>
> Jeremiah 31:3

The Book Of The Law Has Been Canceled And Abolished

God desired for all to go well with the people of Israel throughout all generations (Deuteronomy 5:29). He passionately desired to pour out all his blessings upon them, so many blessings that they could not be counted or contained.

Through the Book of the Law, God established a system of blessings and curses that would motivate the people of Israel to do good, since they would not simply do good because of God's love for them and out of their love for God. Even though they promised God they would obey (Exodus 24:2; Deuteronomy 5:27), they didn't. Consequently, God could never pour out his blessings on them.

Eventually, all the curses of the Book of the Covenant came upon them. Yet, in grace, Jesus took the curse of the law upon himself when he was nailed to the cross. Galatians 3:13 says, *"Christ redeemed us from the curse of the law by becoming a curse for us."* Once nailed to the cross, the Book of the Covenant, or the written code, was canceled and abolished.

> *"When you were dead in your sins...God made you alive with Christ. He forgave us all our sins, having canceled the written code, with its regulations that was against us and that stood opposed to us; he took it away, nailing it to the cross.*
>
> Colossians 2:13-14

> *...abolishing in his flesh the law with its commandments and regulations.*
>
> Ephesians 2:15

It is important to know the Book of the Law (Covenant), or written code, was not the problem. The law is good (Romans 7:12). It reflects the love of God. The problem was with people. They couldn't obey his law (Hebrews 8:7-8). As a result, they would have forever lived under the curse of the law. Thankfully, Jesus not only took upon himself the curse of the law, but God nailed the Book of the Law to the cross with Jesus, canceling and abolishing it forever.

Your Anger Is Toward God

When I teach this truth of grace, some people get mad at me. When the story of God's grace intersects with the story of their lives, they get frustrated with me. But I tell them, *"Your anger really isn't toward me. It is toward God. Because I didn't nail the Book of the Law to the cross with Jesus, God did. I wasn't even around when it happened. I am just telling you what God did."*

God's purpose in doing this was to bring people from every nation together into one family through faith in Jesus where he would be our Father and his Spirit would live in us (Ephesians 2:14-22; Hebrews 8:11).

Those Living Under The Law Are Under A Curse

Even though Jesus took the curse of the law upon himself, setting people free from the Book of the Covenant and its curses, many continued to live according to the law and tried to get others to do the same. This is what was happening in the Galatia. Remember, Paul shared with the people of Galatia the good news of God's grace. They had been set free from the Book of the Law and its curses by grace through faith, but they were allowing the religious leaders to put them back under the law and its curses. They had been running a grace race, but the religious leaders cut in on them, putting them back under the law (Galatians 5:7).

In Paul's letter to the Galatians he told them, *"All who rely on observing the law are under a curse, for it is written: 'Cursed is everyone who does not continue to do everything written in the Book of the Law'"* (Galatians 3:10). He goes on to say that Jesus redeemed us from the law so that we would receive the Spirit of Jesus in us and call God our loving Father (Galatians 4:4-6). By receiving the Spirit of

Jesus, we now experience God's love, joy, peace, patience, kindness, goodness, gentleness, and faithfulness as our Father.

We Have The Same Relationship With God As Jesus Did
God Is Our Loving Father

The relationship we have with God as our loving Father is the same relationship Jesus had with God as his Father. Jesus constantly referred to God as his Father. He was very aware of his Father's love. Jesus said in John 3:35, *"The Father loves the Son…"* He also said in John 14:31, *"…I love the Father…"*

Just before his arrest and crucifixion, Jesus was spending his final hours with his disciples. Jesus told them, *"…the Father himself loves you"* (John 16:27). Then, as he was praying for his disciples, with his arrest and crucifixion drawing near, Jesus prays for his disciples and for all those who would believe in him. This includes you and me. Listen to Jesus praying these words for you:

> *"May they be brought to complete unity to let the*
> *world know that you sent me and have loved them*
> *even as you have loved me…I have made you known*
> *to them, and will continue to make you known in*
> *order that the love you have for me may be in them*
> *and I myself may be in them."*
>
> John 17:20-26

The Father Loves You As Much As He Loves Jesus!

In his prayer, Jesus says the Father loves us with the same love the Father had for him. His prayer was the love the Father had for him would be in you. This is amazing!

God the Father loves you the same way he loves Jesus! Jesus prayed you would experience the Father's love in your heart. He prayed for the story of his Father's love to intersect with the story of your life.

As you read this book, the prayer of Jesus is being answered. You are coming to know, understand, and experience God's love for you as your Father. You are his dearly loved child. Through this realization, you are being set free from the religious system enslaving you. You are being set free from fear, shame, guilt, and condemnation. The story of God's grace is intersecting with the story of your life!

Sharing The Father's Love With The World

Now, as dearly loved children of God, Jesus sends us out as the Father sent him, to share his love and grace with the world (John 20:21). Loved by the Father and by Jesus, we have the wonderful privilege of sharing his love with others, telling them how much God loves them and what he has done by grace to bring them into a relationship with himself. In 2 Corinthians 5:20, Paul says we are ambassadors of the message of grace, speaking on behalf of God himself!

The Spirit-Filled Life

This is the Spirit-filled life. The Spirit-filled life happens when we receive God's grace through faith. God then releases us from the law, or any religious system we have been depending upon to obtain or maintain acceptance with him and sends the Spirit of Jesus to live in us, the Spirit that cries out from within our hearts to God's heart, "*My loving Father. My loving Father who is patient with me, full of joy over me, proud to call me his child, who is not angry with me, who has forgiven me, who is kind to me, good to me, gentle with me, and faithful to me. You will always be full of love to me."* As we experience and enjoy our Father's love, our hearts begin to be filled with his love, joy, peace, patience, kindness, goodness, gentleness, and faithfulness.

Living Under The Influence Of The Father's Love

This is what Ephesians 5:18 means when it says, *"Do not be drunk on wine, but be filled with the Spirit."* To be filled with the Spirit means for us to be intoxicated with our Father's love...to be under the influence of our Father's love so that everything we do and say comes from being under the complete influence of his love. We are filled with our Father's love when we are rooted and established in the immeasurable love Jesus has for us:

> *And I pray that you being rooted and established in*
> *love, may have power together with all the saints, to*
> *grasp how wide and long and high and deep is the*
> *love of Christ, and to know this love that surpasses*
> *knowledge - that you may be filled to the measure of*
> *the fullness of God.*
>
> Ephesians 4:17-19

We have all seen people who become intoxicated when an outside substance enters their bodies and brains. They are not the same people. They do things they would have never done. They say things they would have never said. They become totally different people.

This is what happens when we become intoxicated with our Father's love. We become totally different people! Where we used to create unhappiness in our relationships, we create joy. Where we used to cause problems, we create peace. Where we used to be impatient, we become patient. Where we used to be unkind, we become kind. Where we used to practice immorality, we practice morality. Where we used to do badly, we do good. Where we used to be harsh, we become gentle. Where we used to be unfaithful, we become faithful. Where we once were controlled by anger, we are now controlled by our Father's love. We are intoxicated with our Father's love!

We become intoxicated with our Father's love because we are very aware of our sin. The law has convinced us of the depths of our sin. Yet, through grace, we discover the depths of God's love and forgiveness. We drink in his grace. We drink in his forgiveness. We drink in his love. We drink in his joy. We drink in his patience. We drink in his kindness. We drink in his goodness. We drink in his gentleness. We drink in his faithfulness. Our hearts are now filled with his love. As our hearts are filled with his love, the fruit of his love begins to manifest in our relationships. This is called the fruit of the Spirit (Galatians 5:22-23).

Controlled By The Love Of God

God's heart is for our hearts to be controlled by his love, not by any religious system, not by a law, and not by the Ten Commandments. God has set us free from religious systems, the law, and the Ten Commandments (Galatians 5:1, 13). We are now led by his Spirit (Galatians 5:18).

Freed From The Law So We Can Love

2 Corinthians 3:17 says *"Where the Spirit of the Lord is there is freedom."* The context of this verse is speaking of those who have

come to faith in Jesus and are no longer under the old covenant of law but are under the new covenant of grace. They are no longer under the condemnation of the Ten Commandments (2 Corinthians 3:6-9) but are new creations in whom the Spirit of Jesus lives. They are now "in Christ" (2 Corinthians 3:14).

Because they are in Christ, the old covenant of law is gone, and the new covenant of grace has come (2 Corinthians 5:17). Since Jesus lives in them, which is the meaning of the phrase *where the Spirit of the Lord is*, they are free from the condemnation and rules of their religious system, which is the old covenant known as the Book of the Covenant. They now enjoy a relationship with God as their loving Father. As a result, they are led by the Spirit in love.

God has freed us from the law, not so we can indulge our flesh in sinful living, but so we can impact others by serving them in love, just as Jesus did (Galatians 5:13). By serving others in love, empowered by our Father's love for us and led by the Spirit, the heart of the law is fulfilled. The law reflects God's love and is summed up in this one sentence: "*Love your neighbor as yourself*" (Galatians 5:14). Love is the fulfillment of the law (Romans 13:8-10).

Love Fulfills The Law

Why does love fulfill the law? Because "*love does no harm to its neighbor*" (Romans 13:10). The person living empowered by the love of the Father and led by the Spirit will not commit adultery, murder, steal, covet, dishonor his parents, lie, or break any other commandment of God, since these are harmful to others. We do not break a commandment because there is a law on the outside of us telling us not to do something, but because our Father's love inside of us compels us to love others.

We do not resist stealing because there is a law that says, "Do Not Steal", and if we steal, then we will be under judgment. We do not resist stealing because we want God to bless us. Both are very selfish acts for not stealing. Rather, we do not steal because love does not steal. Instead, love looks for ways to help another person, not hurt them.

Serving One Another In Love

The ultimate act of serving another person in love was when Jesus stepped out of heaven, became human, and humbly took on the nature of a servant. (Philippians 2:6-7). His ultimate act of service in love was when he willfully died on the cross for our sins. This was the greatest act of service ever demonstrated, an act motivated by love...true, selfless, love.

In Jesus, we witness a love that freely gave everything to serve others, receiving nothing in return. This act of selfless love exemplifies what Jesus said about himself in Mark 10:44: *"For even the Son of Man did not come to be served, but to serve, and to give his life as a ransom for many"* (Mark 10:45).

Teaching his twelve disciples to serve others was a major focus for Jesus. His disciples were constantly arguing about who was his greatest disciple (Matthew 22:24) and which disciple would be the greatest in his kingdom (Matthew 18:1). They wanted positions of power when Jesus established God's eternal kingdom on earth. However, Jesus taught them not to be consumed with positions of power but with serving others in love (Mark 10:35-45).

To demonstrate to them the act of serving others in love, he washed their feet. This was his final act of service before his ultimate act of serving the entire world through his death on the cross. The Father put *"all things under his* [Jesus] *power"* (John 13:3). Then

Jesus, the most powerful person on the planet, wrapped a towel around his waist and washed his disciples' feet. He then told his disciples to serve others the same way he served them (John 13:1-15).

It is with this attitude of sacrificial love, empowered by Jesus' love for us and his Spirit in us, that our Father wants us to serve others (Galatians 5:13). The Spirit leads us to serve others in love, unconditional, sacrificial love...even for our enemies...even if it's painful...even if it's costly...even if we receive no benefit, only serving others for their benefit.

Paul taught about this type of love in Philippians 2:5-8. He encouraged the Philippian church to have the mind of Christ. This mind was a servant's mind. It was a mindset that took the attitude of a servant, giving up positions of power, as Jesus did, and taking the place of a lowly servant.

This servant's mindset of Jesus led him to the cross in his ultimate act of service. It is the same mindset we are to have as well. It is a way of thinking, produced by grace, which seeks to serve others rather than being served by others. It is how the Spirit leads us...he leads us to serve others in love, and by serving others in love, we fulfill the law that says, "Love your neighbor as yourself", even though we are not under the law (Galatians 5:13-14).

Looking For Ways To Serve Others In Love

As we grow in our Father's love, we will look for ways to serve others rather than look for ways others can serve us. We will become less angry toward others for not serving us the way we expect. We will become more accepting of one another, looking for ways to express love through acts of service.

By serving others in love, our relationships will become more enjoyable. Our relationships will improve because we will serve more and argue less. As we grow in love, we will stop treating each other with law, judging and condemning each other for not measuring up to one another's standards. Instead, we will serve one another in love. We will focus less on other people meeting our needs, and getting angry when they do not, and more on how we can meet their needs. We will begin to ask, *"What can I do to help them? What can I do to make their lives easier and more enjoyable? What can I do to lighten their load?"*

We will no longer jockey for position to see who is the greatest in our little kingdoms, rather we will take the position that is the greatest in God's kingdom, a position of serving others in love. His powerful kingdom of grace will replace our personal kingdom of greatness.

The Transforming Power Of Love

As we begin to serve others in love, our homes will be transformed. Husbands and wives will remove one another, and their children, from their own "relationship laws", which create judgmental attitudes in the home manifested in anger and arguments. Husbands will begin loving and caring for their wives as Christ loved the family of God through unconditional, sacrificial love demonstrated through acts of service. Wives will respond to their husband's love with respect. Fathers and mothers will begin to see the imperfections in their children, and in one another, not as reasons to get angry but as opportunities to show grace.

These imperfections in one another will become opportunities to show our Father's grace, forgiveness, love, patience, kindness, gentleness, goodness, and faithfulness to each other, leading to joy and peace. When family members fall short because of their sin, the other family members will be filled with grace to them in their sin. In grace-filled homes, families will accept each other's weaknesses and appreciate each other's strengths rather than criticize each other's weaknesses and ignore each other's strengths.

The hearts of children will turn to the hearts of their fathers and mothers. Children will no longer live in fear of a parent's anger but will live filled with a parent's love. Homes of law will be replaced by homes of grace. It's not that grace will create the perfect home, but grace will keep the imperfect home together.

Grace-Based Homes

A law-based home will many times create the appearance of a perfect home because children live in fear of a parent's anger, becoming afraid to disobey. Even though externally the home looks perfect, the hearts of the children are falling apart. Sometimes a grace-based home may look like it is falling apart, but the love and grace being poured into a child's heart by the parents will ultimately empower the child to get his life together.

It's not that grace-filled homes neglect to discipline their children; it's that discipline is administered in an attitude of gentleness and kindness not in harshness and rudeness. I believe this is what it means to raise our children in the training and instruction of the Lord (Ephesians 6:4). Along with teaching them about the Lord's grace, we are to demonstrate his love and grace to them by how we talk to and treat them.

Pouring God's Grace On People

Ephesians 4:31-32 says, *"Get rid of all bitterness, rage and anger, brawling and slander, along with every form of malice. Be kind and compassionate to one another, forgiving each other, just as through Christ God forgave you*." The word for forgiveness and forgave in this verse is the Greek word for grace, *charis*. This verse is telling us to lavish large amounts of grace on others as God lavished upon us through Jesus...to make people the objects of our grace, kindness, compassion, and love rather than our anger and bitterness. As we do this, our relationships will begin to grow in the soil of God's grace and Satan's grip on our relationships will be released (Ephesians 4:26-29).

When teaching under law to convince people of their need for grace, Jesus taught his disciples that if a person does not forgive another person, then God will not forgive the one withholding forgiveness. He said that if we do not forgive others their sins against us, then our Father will not forgive our sins (Matthew 6:12, 14-15). This was before the new covenant of grace. Now that grace has come, which is Jesus' payment for all our sins through his death, we forgive others the same way God has forgiven us. We will take a closer look at the new covenant in chapter eleven.

But for now, remember, the law seeks to motivate the selfish hearts of mankind through blessings and curses, ultimately showing us our need for grace. Jesus, teaching under law, seeks to motivate a person to forgive another person in the same way by saying unless we forgive, God will not forgive us; thus, leading them to an awareness of their need for grace. But after the cross, and through our awareness of sin and acceptance of grace, our motivation to forgive others comes from the grace lavished upon us by God through Jesus when he forgave us all our sins.

Pouring God's Love On People

After the teaching in Ephesians 4:31-32, which encourages us to give to others the same grace God has given to us, Ephesians 5:1-2 teaches us, as God's dearly loved children, to love others as God loves us and to live a life of sacrificial love toward others, just as Christ loved us.

It was this kind of love, grace, compassion, kindness, and forgiveness that Jesus spoke about during the *Sermon on the Mount*, which we learned about in chapter five. It was a love that showed grace to those mistreating us and grace to our enemies by treating them kindly, praying for them, serving them, and greeting them (Luke 6:27-36). It was love and grace in action. Now, the love, grace, compassion, kindness, and forgiveness God has given us in our sins becomes the power to show love, grace, compassion, kindness, and forgiveness to others in their sins.

Jesus Pours Out Grace And Love From The Cross

Jesus demonstrated the Father's grace when he looked down from the cross on those who mistreated him, saying, *"Father, forgive them, for they do not know what they are doing"* (Luke 23:34). Through this act of grace, he fulfilled the words he taught in the *Sermon on the Mount*: *"Love your enemies, and pray for those who persecute* [mistreat] *you"* (Matthew 5:44). These are words we never could fulfill but were required to fulfill if we were to gain entrance into God's kingdom. However, the words we could never fulfill Jesus fulfilled for us, and by doing so, he became the perfect sacrifice for our sins. He was the perfect sacrifice because he represented the Father's grace.

No Law Can Produce This Kind Of Transformation

As we grow in our Father's love, grace, compassion, kindness, and forgiveness, we will be transformed into people who demonstrate our Father's love, grace, compassion, kindness, and forgiveness to others, even to our enemies. No law or religious system can produce this kind of internal transformation in a person's heart. Only the love of God poured into our hearts can produce this kind of change. This is the Spirit-filled life (2 Corinthians 3:17-18).

10

The Story Of God's Love And Forgiveness

Our need for forgiveness goes back to Adam in the Garden of Eden. God told Adam if he ate from the tree, he would die. As we know, he ate from the tree. This disobedience to God, to his love, is called sin. The penalty for sin is death (Romans 6:23). Through Adam, sin and death spread to the entire human race (Romans 5:12). Consequently, we were in need of forgiveness for our sins and in need of life because of death. God, because he loves us so much, provided the grace all of us need to experience his forgiveness through the death of Jesus and then provided eternal life to us through the resurrection of Jesus (Romans 5:12-21).

God Is Not Counting Our Sins Against Us!

2 Corinthians 5:18-19 says, *"All this is from God, who reconciled us to himself through Christ and gave us the ministry of reconciliation: that God was reconciling the world to himself in Christ, not counting men's sins against them."*

Understanding these verses on forgiveness totally changed my life. For most of my life, I thought God was counting my sins against me. I was taught I needed to daily ask God to forgive me for my sins. So day after day and year after year, I continued to ask God to forgive me. When asking God to forgive me, I felt good for a moment. But the next day, I felt guilty...so what did I do? I asked God to forgive me again. I did this repetitively for years, continually being tormented by guilt, never realizing God was no longer counting my sins against me. Had I understood God was no longer counting my sins against me, as these verses show, I would have stopped asking for his forgiveness and would have spent those days and years freed from guilt, thanking him I was completely forgiven.

All Our Sins Were Counted Against Jesus

2 Corinthians 5:18-19 says plainly that God is not counting our sins against us. But why not? Why is God not counting our sins against us? God is not counting our sins against us because they were all counted against Jesus. If all our sins were counted against Jesus, then how many of our sins are left to be counted against us? None!

When Jesus died for our sins, he died for all our sins. Our past, our present, and our future sins were all paid for by Jesus. Romans 5:8 says, *"But God demonstrates his own love for us in this: While we were yet sinners, Christ died for us."* How many of our sins did Jesus die for? He died for all our sins. All our sins were in the future when Jesus died. This means the sins we have yet to commit have already been paid for by Jesus!

The payment for our sins by Jesus is called grace! Hebrews 2:9 says, *"...by the grace of God he* [Jesus] *might taste death for everyone."* Ephesians 1:6-8 says, *"...to the praise of his glorious grace, which he has freely given us in the One he loves. In him* [Jesus] *we have redemption through his blood, the forgiveness of sins in accordance with the riches of God's grace that he lavished on us with all wisdom and understanding."*

God, in his love, wisdom, and understanding moved in grace to have Jesus die in our place by shedding his blood for all our sins. He died for everyone and for every sin. His shed blood was the full payment and brought complete forgiveness for our sins. This is called redemption.

Redemption is being totally set free from the payment of sin, which is death, because Jesus paid our sin debt in full when he died in our place. Redemption is also being made forever alive through his resurrection, which is eternal life.

Redemption, then, is Jesus undoing everything Adam did. God, through Jesus, lavished his grace upon us, forgiving us for all our sins, restoring us to life...eternal life, and reconciling us to himself in a love relationship. We have become the objects of his abundant grace!

We Receive God's Forgiveness By Faith

Ephesians 2:8-9 says, *"It is by grace we have been saved through faith - and this not from yourselves, it is the gift of God - not by works, so that no one can boast."* It is by faith that we receive the gift of forgiveness and eternal life provided by grace. By grace, through faith, we have been saved from death and brought into an eternal relationship with God, which is life.

Only Grace Removes Guilt

Good works can never pay the death penalty for sin, only grace can. A person can try to be good for the rest of his life, but he is still guilty before God for his sins. His good works will not pay his sin penalty. For example, someone on death row can promise to be a good prisoner for the entire time he is on death row but being good will not make up for the crime he committed. The penalty must still be paid.

Good Works Do Not Remove Guilt

Similarly, our good works can never pay our penalty for sin. The penalty for sin is death. Obedience to the law can never pay this penalty. Religious activity and morality can never pay our sin penalty. No matter how good a person appears, God knows their sinful thoughts and deeds. These sinful thoughts and deeds are under the penalty of death. The penalty must be paid. The good news of grace is that God, through Jesus, fully paid the penalty for us and gave us forgiveness and eternal life as a gift.

A gift is something someone purchases for us with their own money and then gives us to enjoy. Through the blood of Jesus, God purchased for us forgiveness and eternal life. He then gives us these gifts to enjoy. We do not work for these gifts. We cannot earn these gifts. They are free gifts of grace. We receive them by faith in Jesus.

For many years, I could not enjoy God's gift of forgiveness. I thought God dispensed his forgiveness to me in daily doses based upon my daily confession of sin. But then he opened my eyes to see that forgiveness was his gift of grace to me, which he wanted me to enjoy. His gift of forgiveness was free, full, and forever, purchased by the blood of Jesus and received simply by faith. Now I enjoy daily his gift of forgiveness. Since this time, my life has never been the same!

God wants you to enjoy his gift of forgiveness, too! If you have been living in bondage because of the misunderstanding that God gives out forgiveness in daily doses based upon daily confession of sin, you no longer have to live this way. You can start daily enjoying God's gift of forgiveness by faith, which is simply accepting God's gift through faith in Jesus.

God Loves Us And Paid Our Sin Penalty For Us

God's payment for our sins through Jesus and his purchase of the gifts of forgiveness and eternal life were motivated by his great love for us. We have already seen Romans 5:8 which says, *"But God demonstrates his love for us in this: While we were still sinners, Christ died for us." 1 John 4:9-10 says, "In this the love of God was made manifest among us, that God sent his only Son into the world, so that we might live through him. In this is love, not that we have loved God but that he loved us and sent his Son to be the propitiation for our sins."* (English Standard Version)

Some versions of the Bible use the words *atoning sacrifice or the word atonement* in the place of the word propitiation in 1 John 4:10. The word atone means to cover. Jesus did not atone for our sins, or cover the payment for our sins, he completely paid our sin penalty, taking it away forever! The better word to describe this payment is *propitiation*, meaning to completely take away our sin penalty by fully paying it on our behalf. Jesus just did not cover our sin penalty, he paid it in full! We will look further into this in chapter eleven.

How much does God love you? He loves you so much that he sent his one and only Son into the world to pay your sin penalty. He loves you! Look at what Jesus says in John 3:16-17: *"For God so loved the world that he gave his one and only Son, that whoever believes in him should not perish but have everlasting life. For God did not send his Son into the world to condemn the world, but to save the world through him."*

We Enter God's Eternal Kingdom By Believing

You are the object of God's unconditional love! In this verse, Jesus tells us God loved the people of the world so much that he gave his one and only Son to save them. The world is filled with people who have sinned greatly, myself included. Yet, in love, God sent Jesus to save us from our sins, not to condemn us for our sins. How do we receive God's love revealed through Jesus? How do we receive salvation? How do we receive eternal life? According to Jesus, by believing.

To Believe Means To Receive

So, what does it mean to believe? John 1:12 says, *"Yet to all to who received him, to those who believed in his name, he gave the right to become children of God."* To believe means to receive Jesus. So how do we receive Jesus? By faith. By faith we are saved. We are saved by trusting Jesus, not by trying earnestly. We are saved by believing, not by behaving morally. We are saved by faith, not by following religious rules and rituals.

Maybe you have been seeking to save yourself by trying earnestly, behaving morally, and following rules and rituals religiously. But now, the story of God's grace is intersecting with the story of your life, and you are realizing salvation is not earned by your good works but is received by grace through faith.

Nicodemus: From Achieving To Believing

One who came to this realization was a man named Nicodemus. Nicodemus was a Pharisee who thought salvation, or entering God's eternal kingdom, was achieved through trying earnestly to follow the Law of Moses, behaving morally, and following rules and rituals. He heard about Jesus and wanted to talk with him further about entering God's kingdom. He knew he could not have a sincere conversation with Jesus during the day because during the day the other Pharisees were always trying to trap and trick Jesus. So to have a genuine conversation with Jesus, he approached Jesus at night (John 3:1-2).

On the heart of Nicodemus was the same question everyone else had, *"What does it take to enter God's kingdom and have everlasting life?"* Even though he did not directly ask Jesus this question, Jesus knew what was on his heart. So Jesus brought up the subject. He told Nicodemus, *"I tell you the truth. No one can see the kingdom of God unless he is born again"* (John 3:3).

The term *born again* was confusing to Nicodemus. So, to clarify, Jesus told him no one can enter the kingdom of God unless he is born of water and the Spirit (John 3:5). By this, Jesus was saying not only does one need to be born physically, born of the water, but must also be born spiritually, born of the Spirit. Nicodemus was curious about how a person could be born of the Spirit. Jesus told him he must be born again by believing (John 3:14-16). He told Nicodemus it is by believing one is born spiritually, or where the Spirit comes to live in the heart of a person, enabling him to live eternally in the kingdom of God.

In their conversation, Jesus emphasized the necessity of believing. Jesus told him, *"For God so loved the world that he sent his one and only Son, that whosoever believes in him shall not perish but have eternal life. For God did not send his Son into the world to condemn the world, but to save the world through him"* (John 3:16-17).

Believing was contrary to Nicodemus' entire belief system as a Pharisee. As we have learned, Pharisees thought for one to enter God's kingdom, he needed to behave morally. By behaving morally, one would qualify to enter the kingdom. Now Jesus is telling him it is by believing, not by behaving, that one enters God's kingdom. Jesus is turning his whole belief system upside down.

Nicodemus' Concept Of God

Not only was Nicodemus' concept of entering God's kingdom wrong, but according to Jesus, his view of God was wrong too! Jesus told Nicodemus that God loved the people of the world. *"How could that be?"*, Nicodemus wondered.

As a Pharisee, Nicodemus was convinced God hated sinners, tax collectors, prostitutes, and those like them in the world. *"Surely"*, he thought, *"God doesn't love them. He doesn't love sinners. He loves people like me. He loves people who obey the Ten Commandments. He loves people who behave morally. He loves people who follow religious rules and rituals. And now Jesus is telling me God loves everybody! He is telling me God's heart is not to condemn the people of the world but to save them, so they will not perish but have eternal life. And whoever believes, even the sinner, prostitute, and tax collector, is saved from perishing and will be a part of God's eternal kingdom."*

The belief that God did not desire to condemn anyone but loved everyone, offering eternal life to all who believed, totally shattered Nicodemus' entire belief system. The very foundation by which Nicodemus lived as a Pharisee was now being dismantled by Jesus in one conversation. The story of God's grace was intersecting with the story of his life. What would he do with this grace? He was at a crisis of faith. Would he receive the words of Jesus by believing, or would he reject the words of Jesus, continuing to try to behave his way into the kingdom of God?

Nicodemus Believes

We find later in the Bible Nicodemus defending Jesus among the Pharisees (John 7:50-52). Then, following Jesus' death, he joins Joseph of Arimathea in preparing his body for burial (John 19:38-42). Through these actions, I believe Nicodemus received the grace Jesus was offering him in their conversation. He believed! He went from trying to enter God's kingdom to trusting in Jesus. When his life intersected with the story of God's grace, his life was never the same!

What About You?

Maybe this is you. Maybe you have been trying earnestly to achieve salvation, to enter God's eternal kingdom. Maybe you thought by behaving morally you would earn eternal life, gaining entrance into God's kingdom. Maybe you were taught it is by following religious rules and rituals you are saved. Maybe you were taught it is through commitment and faithfulness to a certain religious organization or denomination that you are saved. But now, God's story of grace is intersecting with the story of your life, and you are beginning to question your beliefs. I understand.

I have been where you are. I know the crisis of faith you are facing. Do you place your faith in God's word or will you continue to place your faith in the words of men? To place your faith in God's word, trusting in Jesus alone for salvation, feels wrong to you emotionally. But in your heart, you know it is right spiritually. I want to encourage you to place your faith in God's word. It is by grace you are saved through faith (Ephesians 2:8-9).

You Can Receive God's Forgiveness By Faith

It is through placing our faith in Jesus that we experience God's forgiveness. Paul, in Acts 13:38-39, says, *"Therefore, my brothers, I want you to know through Jesus the forgiveness of sins is proclaimed to you. Through him everyone who believes is justified from everything you could not be justified by the law of Moses."*

In Acts 26:18, when Paul recounts his Damascus road experience with the ascended Jesus, Jesus tells Paul that he is sending him to tell others to receive forgiveness. Jesus says to Paul, *"I am sending you...so they may receive forgiveness of sins..."*

Forgiveness does not come by following the requirements of a religious or moral system, such as the Law of Moses, or any other system. Forgiveness cannot be earned. Forgiveness is received by faith in Jesus Christ. We receive God's forgiveness the moment we believe.

We Don't Ask God For Forgiveness

Notice in the previous verses, Paul proclaims the forgiveness of sins through what Jesus did for us on the cross. Notice what he is asking people to do. Paul is asking people to receive God's forgiveness through belief in Jesus. Notice what he is not asking people to do. He is not asking people to ask God to forgive them. Rather, Paul is now an ambassador of what Jesus did on the cross. God is making his appeal through Paul (2 Corinthians 5:18-21). God, through Paul, is asking people to accept his forgiveness through belief in Jesus. And when people believe, they are justified, meaning they are declared by God to be innocent in his sight.

In their denominational, organizational, and religious systems, people are taught they need to ask God to forgive them. They are taught to see God as withholding his forgiveness until they ask him for it, while the entire time, God is holding his forgiveness out to them.

This is the good news Paul was proclaiming to his hearers, *"God is holding his forgiveness out to you!"* On behalf of God, Paul is asking his audience to accept, through belief in Jesus, the forgiveness God is holding out to them.

God doesn't want you to keep asking him to forgive you, as if he is holding back his forgiveness. He doesn't want you living in this religious bondage. Because God loves you so much, he longs for you to enjoy the forgiveness he is freely and fully holding out to you in Jesus. The desire of God's heart is for you to accept through faith the forgiveness he is holding out to you.

I know this sounds different than probably anything you have heard concerning forgiveness. It was different for me. I understand. But rather than placing my faith in what I had previously heard, I put my faith in God's word. At this point in my life, I stopped seeing God as a god who was withholding forgiveness from me, only granting forgiveness to me when I asked, and started seeing him as the God who was holding out his forgiveness to me, and all I needed to do was accept his forgiveness through belief in Jesus.

All Your Sins Are Forgiven

How much of God's forgiveness do we receive when we believe? We receive all his forgiveness! Colossians 2:13-14 says, *"When you were dead in your sins...God made you alive with Christ. He forgave us all our sins, having canceled the written code...nailing it to the cross."* It only makes sense that if Jesus died for all our sins, then he would forgive us for all our sins.

You Have Been Made Alive

Notice the connection between forgiveness and being made alive with Christ. Remember, sin caused death. Jesus died for all our sins. When we believe, we experience God's forgiveness of all our sins, then, through the resurrection of Jesus, we are made alive with him. If all our sins aren't forgiven, then we could not be made alive with Christ but would remain spiritually dead, disconnected from a love relationship with God. Similarly, if we must confess our sins for forgiveness every time we sin, then each time we sin we would die, because the penalty for sin is death, thus severing our relationship with God with each sin. For us to be made alive with Christ, having an unending relationship with God, then all our sins must be forgiven. That's what God did...he forgave all our sins!

But What About…?

Whenever I teach what God's word says about complete forgiveness in Christ, where we don't ask God to keep forgiving us, but we accept through faith in Jesus God's complete forgiveness for all of our sins for all time, I am typically asked the following questions, *"What about 1 John 1:9?"*, *"What about The Lord's Prayer?"*, and *"What about 2 Chronicles 7:14?"*.

These are all very good questions, needing to be answered. Later in this chapter, I will address the question on 1 John 1:9. Already, in chapter nine, we addressed forgiveness as it relates to *The Lord's Prayer*, seeing that *The Lord's Prayer* is under the old covenant of law, rather than the new covenant of grace.

So, for now, let's look at 2 Chronicles 7:14 which says, *"if my people, who are called by my name, will humble themselves and pray and seek my face and turn from their wicked ways, then I will hear from heaven, and I will forgive their sin and will heal their land."*

This verse is to be understood in the same way as *The Lord's Prayer*. 2 Chronicles 7:14 is in the old covenant of law. The new covenant of grace had not yet come. Jesus had not died for the sins of the world when God said this.

It is important to know who God is speaking to in this verse. He is speaking to the nation of Israel who is still under the old covenant of law. At this time, the people of Israel were under the curses of the law because they turned away from God in disobedience, and he is telling them he will hear and forgive them if they humble themselves, pray, seek his face, and turn from their wicked ways.

Bible teachers who don't understand the difference between the old and new covenants will seek to apply this verse to believers in Jesus who are now living under the new covenant of grace.

However, this verse does not apply to new covenant believers. We are now a part of the body of Christ. The old covenant of law was nailed with Jesus to the cross and has now been abolished (Ephesians 2:14-16; Colossians 2:13-14). All our sins have been forgiven. God has made one new family of grace out of the Jews and Gentiles. Each time someone places his or her faith in Jesus, God places that person into the family of grace.

In the family of grace, unlike the people of Israel who were living under law, we are already forgiven for all our sins (Colossians 2:13), and now we forgive one another as the Lord forgave us.

> *Bear with each other and forgive one another if any of you has a grievance against someone. Forgive as the Lord forgave you.*
>
> Colossians 3:13

Prideful People Reject God's Grace

In a previous chapter, I shared that many people get angry at me when I teach the truth of grace which says God nailed the written code to the cross, canceling its regulations, and abolishing it forever. These same people become angry with me when I teach the truths of grace that God is not counting our sins against us and that he has forgiven all our sins. I tell them the same thing, *"Your anger is not toward me. I am not the one who said God is not counting our sins against us. I am not the one who said all our sins have been forgiven. God spoke these truths. I just have the great privilege of being an ambassador of this good news. Your anger is not toward me, it's toward God."*

Typically, these same people teach something the Bible does not teach. They teach there are two types of forgiveness: *positional* and *relational*. They teach positional forgiveness is that God has forgiven all our sins. Yet, daily, we must ask for God's forgiveness from a relationship standpoint. This makes no sense.

I love what Bob George said when speaking on the absurdity of positional and relational forgiveness. Looking up, as if looking up at Jesus suffering on the cross, Bob shouted, *"Hey Jesus, are you dying for positional or relational forgiveness?"*

The truth, according to the Bible, is that Jesus died for forgiveness. There is no such teaching in the Bible, none, about positional and relational forgiveness, none at all! Forgiveness is forgiveness. When God declared you forgiven, and when you, by faith, received his forgiveness, it was forgiveness for all your sins for all time.

Humble People Receive God's Grace

I have also noticed there are those who do not get angry with me when I teach the truths of God's grace. They are the humble...the broken...the poor in spirit. Those who are very aware of their sins. These are the ones who receive God's grace with an appreciative heart. These are the ones, when the story of God's grace intersects with the story of their lives, who are set free from guilt, shame, and condemnation, experiencing life-change the very moment they believe!

The Kingdom Of The Forgiven

The very moment we believe, God takes us out of the kingdom of guilt, shame, and condemnation and places us into the Kingdom of the Forgiven. Colossians 1:13-14 says, *"For he has rescued us from the dominion of darkness and brought us into the kingdom of the Son he loves, in whom we have redemption, the forgiveness of sins."* God, because of his great love for us, has rescued us from being ruled by the darkness of our sin, shame, guilt, and condemnation. Through his grace, our sins have been forgiven, and now we live in the kingdom of Jesus...the Kingdom of the Forgiven.

Citizens of the Kingdom

For those who have placed their faith in Jesus, we are citizens of the Kingdom of the Forgiven, where Jesus is the Savior-King. It is Jesus who became our Savior by dying for our sins, so we could become citizens of his kingdom. This is how much Jesus loves you! He loves you so much that he, the King, would become your Savior so you could become a citizen of his kingdom...welcome to the Kingdom of the Forgiven!

Preoccupation With Ourselves Makes Us Miserable

Many of those who have placed their faith in Jesus, becoming citizens of his kingdom, do not enjoy the forgiveness that has been freely given to them. They constantly are asking God to forgive them of their sins. One day they feel forgiven, the next day they don't. As stated earlier in this chapter, I did this for years as a Christian, constantly asking God to forgive me...trying to stay forgiven by following the rules of the religious system I had been taught. Rather than being taught all that God has done for me through Jesus to secure my forgiveness and fellowship with him, I was taught all the things I needed to do to stay forgiven and in fellowship with him.

I was taught I should have no "unconfessed sins" in my life if I was to "stay forgiven and in fellowship with God". To "stay in fellowship with God", I was taught I needed to daily "keep short accounts on sin" by confessing my sins and asking for God's forgiveness. By doing this, I could be sure my fellowship with God would not be broken. I didn't want unbroken fellowship with God. As a result, I became preoccupied with myself...with my sin...trying to "keep short accounts on sins", yet always wondering and worrying if I had any "unconfessed sins" in my life. Had I missed any sins? I constantly worried if I was "in fellowship" or "out of fellowship with God". What a miserable way to live!

Preoccupation with ourselves and our sins definitely does not lead to the abundant life Jesus came for us to experience! As Bob George says in his book, *Classic Christianity*, *"Preoccupation with ourselves makes us miserable."* I was one miserable person!

Preoccupation with ourselves leads to one of two things: pride-*look at how great I am doing in my religious and moral system*, or pity-*look at how bad I am doing in my religious or moral system*. For me, I lived more on the side of self-pity, never feeling like I could measure up to the requirements of the religious and moral system I had embraced. I certainly wasn't enjoying my relationship with God, since I was constantly wondering if I was "in fellowship with God" or "out of fellowship with God".

How The Misinterpretation Of 1 John 1:9 Kept Me Preoccupied With Myself

The verse most Bible teachers refer to when teaching people to "stay forgiven and in fellowship with God by keeping short accounts on their sins" is 1 John 1:9. 1 John 1:9 says, *"If we confess our sins he is faithful and just to forgive us of our sins and cleanse us from all unrighteousness."* This was the verse emphasized to me more than any other verse by the leaders within the religious system I had come to embrace. At this point in my life, I did not realize I needed to compare the words of others with God's word. I just assumed what they were teaching was correct and this is what I needed to do.

But after God's revelation of grace to me through *Classic Christianity*, I realized I needed to evaluate the words of people with the word of God, the Bible. It wasn't just important to know what a verse says but to actually find out what it means. I was familiar with what most commentaries and study Bible notes said about 1 John 1:9. All the ones I read said the same thing: *To stay in fellowship with God, we must daily confess our sins*.

1 John 1:9 in Context

I began to study 1 John 1:9 in context. I read through the book many times to get an understanding of the issues John was addressing. One of the issues was that of forgiveness and fellowship with God. However, in my studies, I saw he was addressing the issue of forgiveness and fellowship with God concerning false teachers seeking to lead believers in Jesus astray from truth (1 John 2:26), and he was not addressing the issue of believers staying forgiven and in fellowship with God through continual confession of sin.

John Wrote To Protect People From False Teachers Claiming To Be In Fellowship With God

In 1 John 1:1-5, John said he was in fellowship with God, or had knowledge of the truth, because he spent time with Jesus. Since he spent time with Jesus, he had an understanding of truth these false teachers did not have. If his readers could trust anyone, it would be John, rather than the false teachers making erroneous claims they were in fellowship with God by claiming to possess the knowledge of the truth about God and eternal life.

In John 1, John was not writing to provide a religious system by which believers can stay forgiven and in fellowship with God, as many Bible teachers and commentaries proclaim. Instead, he was writing to protect believers from being led astray by false teachers and the religious system these teachers were falsely proclaiming about how to know God and possess eternal life.

These false teachers, infiltrating the church John was writing to, claimed to be in fellowship with God, know the truth, and have knowledge of eternal life. But they denied they had sinned and that Jesus was the Christ. They were claiming to be in the light by having spiritual knowledge about God, but in their denial of personal sin and Jesus being the Son of God, the Christ, they were making God out to be a liar (1 John 1:10, 5:9-10). They were making God a liar because God said, *"All have sinned"* (Romans 3:23). They were also making God a liar because God's testimony was Jesus is the Christ (John 5:37). By these denials, all of which are contrary to the Christian faith, they were in the darkness, even though they were claiming to be in the light, or in fellowship with God.

John, therefore, communicates one of the foundational truths of Christianity in 1 John 1:9 which says, *"If we* [sinful members of the human race] *confess our sins* [admit we have sinned], *he is faithful and just* [God will do would he said he will do based upon what Jesus has already done for us through his blood] *to forgive us our sins and purify us from all unrighteousness."*

We Experience Forgiveness And Righteousness The Moment We Believe

So, when do we experience the forgiveness of God and become righteous before God? The moment we believe! This verse is not for believers in need of "staying forgiven or in fellowship with God by keeping short accounts on sin". That is not at all the context of 1 John 1:9. Rather, it is the statement of scriptural truth in comparison to the denial of personal sin by the false teachers.

John Wrote To People Whose Sins Had Been Forgiven

It is important to know that John was actually writing to those whose sins had been forgiven, because these false teachers were trying to convince them they had not been forgiven! 1 John 2:12 says, *"I write to you dear children because your sins have been forgiven on account of his name."* Every time John used the phrase *"I write to you"* it was to expose the religious beliefs of the false teachers and to confirm the truths the believers had already been taught (1 John 2:20-21). And what was the truth they had been taught? When you place your faith in Jesus, you receive all of God's forgiveness!

Those In The Darkness Were False Teachers Claiming To Know God

Obviously, those John addressed as being in the darkness and not in fellowship with God were not believers in Jesus, but they were false teachers who claimed to know God, yet denied the essential truths of Christianity, which were they had sinned (1 John 1:8), and that Jesus is the Christ (1 John 2:22-23).

Pharisaical Teachings Had Infiltrated The Church

What is interesting is the same words John used to identify the beliefs and claims of false teachers infiltrating the church are the same words Jesus used to identify the false beliefs and teachings of the Pharisees. Jesus told the Pharisees that even though they claimed to know God and be in fellowship with him, the truth was not in them and they were liars (John 8:55). He told them they did not know God, even though they claimed they did (John 7:28; 8:19, 54-55; 15:21). They were in the darkness, since they did not believe Jesus was the Christ (John 8:12-13; 12:46). These were the very same denials of those infiltrating the church John wrote to, which leads us to believe that a Pharisaical religious system was being propagated by the false teachers and John was writing to expose their system and beliefs.

The False Teachers Couldn't Love

These false teachers John was writing about had the same problem the Pharisees had in Jesus' time. Though they claimed to know God, the love of God was not in their hearts (John 5:42; Matthew 22:34-40). They were very hateful people. John asks how they can really know God, since God is love. If they really knew God, they would know God is love, resulting in loving others (1 John 4:7-8). However, their concept of God was not one of love and forgiveness for sinners but one of condemnation and judgment.

As the false teachings of those claiming to know God spread, those who previously believed on the name of Jesus lost their confidence in God's love and forgiveness and were now living in terror of God's punishment (1 John 4:16-18). So, John wrote to remind them of God's love displayed when Jesus fully paid their sin debt through his death. This perfect love demonstrated through Jesus' death casts out all fear of punishment and condemnation from God for those who believe (1 John 4:18).

John wrote to remind his readers to rely on God's love for them (1 John 4:16) rather than be manipulated by the false teachers who were denying Jesus was the Son of God, who had no love in their hearts for others (1 John 4:20-21), and who were stealing the confidence of the believers by terrorizing them with the inaccurate teaching of God's judgment, totally dismissing the truth of Jesus' death as full payment for the debt for our sin (1 John 2:1-2, 4:7-5:5). No wonder John said they were liars, in the darkness, and the truth of God's word was not in them (1 John 1:6, 8, 10; 2:4, 9-11; 22-23).

The False Teachers Were Making God Out To Be A Liar

Many Bible teachers claim that 1 John 1:10 refers to believers in Jesus who were making God out to be a liar by denying they had sinned. They say 1 John 1:10 is about believers whom God's word does not live. My question, concerning this interpretation of 1 John 1:10, is how can John be referring to believers in 1 John 1:10 when he says in 1 John 2:14 that the word is living in believers?

In my understanding of this verse, 1 John 1:10 is not referring to believers who are out of fellowship with God but to false teachers claiming to be in fellowship with God, or know God, yet seeking to lead believers away from the truth of God.

Jesus told the Pharisees they had no room for his word in their hearts (John 8:37) and God's word did not live in them (John 5:38). This seems to be exactly what John was saying. Yet in many commentaries and study Bible notes, 1 John 1:6, 8, and 10 refer to those John addressed as believers rather than false teachers.

The False Teachers Taught More Than Belief Was Needed To Possess Eternal Life

These false teachers were also teaching that eternal life was something more than simply believing in Jesus. Evidently, they were teaching the believers that a person had to participate in their religious system for eternal life. As a result, they were confused. They were uncertain if they had eternal life. So, John wrote to correct the false teaching causing confusion among the believers. He says in 1 John 5:11-13, *"God has given us eternal life, and this life is in the Son. He who has the Son has life; he who does not have the Son of God does not have life. I write these things to you who believe in the name of the Son of God so that you may know you have eternal life."*

John cuts through all the religious requirements for salvation being promoted among the believers by these false teachers and states that eternal life is in a person, Jesus. He says eternal life is not gained by participating in a religious system but is given to us in Jesus when we believe.

John concludes his letter by saying, *"We also know that the Son of God has come and has given us understanding, so that we may know him who is true - and we are in him who is true-even in his Son Jesus Christ. He is the true God and eternal life* (1 John 5:20).

No Religious System Needed For Eternal Life

Maybe like me, you fell into a religious system, trying to maintain God's forgiveness by practicing religious, denominational, or organizational rituals or requirements. Maybe you fell into a system, trying to avoid God's punishment by following these rituals and requirements. Maybe you live daily trying to stay in fellowship with God, but you secretly wonder if you are in fellowship with him. Maybe you live daily terrified of God's judgment. Maybe you were manipulated into thinking that by faithfully participating in a certain religious organization you could gain eternal life.

I have good news for you! If you have come to faith in Jesus, if you believe on his name, you have received God's forgiveness and you have eternal life. His perfect love fully paid your sin penalty, completely removing you from judgment. You can be confident you are loved and forgiven. You are in the truth. His word lives in you. You are in fellowship with God. You are in the light. The story of God's love and forgiveness has intersected with the story of your life. This is the story of the New Covenant. This is the story of grace!

11

The Story Of The New Covenant

Many people have been taught and believe the New Covenant, or New Testament, starts at Matthew chapter one. Why would they believe differently? This traditional teaching within denominations and organizations, having been passed down from generation to generation, is widely accepted as truth. To believe something different would feel wrong. To teach anything different would be to open oneself up to great criticism among others. But we can't be controlled by others' words about us. Rather, we must be compelled by the word of God written for us. So, what does the word of God say concerning when the New Testament begins?

Where Does The New Testament Begin?
The Bible teaches the New Testament, or New Covenant, doesn't start with Matthew chapter one but with Matthew chapter twenty-seven, the death of Jesus. As a matter of fact, the Bible teaches the New Testament was not in effect before Jesus died, but it went into effect when he shed his blood for the forgiveness of our sins through his death.

> *...the blood of Christ...*[Jesus] *offered himself unblemished to God...Christ the mediator of a new covenant...in the case of a will* [testament or covenant] *it is necessary to prove the death of the one who made it, because a will* [testament or covenant] *is in force only when somebody has died; it*

never takes effect while the one who made it is living.
That is why the first covenant [Book of the Covenant]
was not put into effect without blood.
Hebrews 9:14-18

The Death Of Jesus Ushered In The New Covenant of Grace

It was the blood of animals that ushered in the old covenant [testament] of law (Hebrews 9:18-22). According to Jesus, it was his own blood that ushered in the new covenant [testament] of grace (Matthew 26:27-28; Luke 22:19-20). It was his blood, not his birth, which began the new covenant. The question is: Whose words will we believe? Will we believe the words of others or the words of the Bible and Jesus? The words of teachers, as stated by Jesus, can nullify God's word (Mark 7:13) if what is traditional is allowed to replace what is biblical.

Rather than accepting the words of teachers as truth, let's evaluate their words with God's word, then allow God's word to determine what is true. Once we know the truth, the truth will set us free.

Eat And Drink Of The New Covenant

Just before his arrest and crucifixion, Jesus was having his last supper with his disciples. Taking bread, he broke it, saying, *"Take and eat; this is my body"* (Matthew 26:26). *"This is my body given for you; do this in remembrance of me"* (Luke 22:19). Then, taking the cup, he said *"This cup is the new covenant* [testament] *in my blood poured out for you"* (Luke 22:20). *"Drink from it, all of you. This is my blood of the covenant poured out for many for the forgiveness of sins"* (Matthew 26:27-28).

The bread his disciples ate represented the complete payment Jesus would make for the sins of the world by giving his body on the cross for our sin payment. The cup represented God's total forgiveness given to us through the blood of Jesus. Together, Jesus called this the new covenant, or the new testament.

Jesus tells us to eat and drink from the new covenant. We eat and drink of the new covenant by faith. By faith, we eat and drink of his grace...his love...his forgiveness...his resurrection. Since the new covenant is what Jesus tells us to eat of and drink from, then it is vital we understand the new covenant.

Understanding the subject of the new covenant is essential to enjoying our relationship with God. Once the story of the new covenant intersects with the story of our lives, we will enjoy our relationship with God in a way we never imagined. So, let's take a closer look at the story of the new covenant.

Before There Was A New Covenant, There Was An Old Covenant

For there to be a new covenant, there had to be an old covenant. The old covenant was the covenant of law, the Book of the Covenant, that God gave the people of Israel through Moses to govern their relationship with himself (Exodus 24:7; Deuteronomy 28:58). It contained the regulations needed for the forgiveness of sins for the people through the sacrificial offerings of the blood of animals.

Animals Were Sacrificed For Sins

Remember, the penalty for sin is death. When Adam and Eve sinned in the Garden of Eden, rather paying the penalty for their own sins, which was death, an innocent animal died in their place. The animal was sacrificed for their sins. This practice of animal sacrifice for the sins of people continued. After Israel became a nation, an animal sacrificial system was put into place and was contained in the Book of the Covenant. We know this book as the Old Covenant, or Old Testament.

The Tent And Temple

To carry out the animal sacrifices of the old covenant, a tent or tabernacle was created. Later, it was built into a temple. The presence of God among the people was represented by the temple. The blueprint for the original tent and its furnishings was given directly by God to Moses (Exodus 25:8-9). The priests managed the tent and all its animal sacrifices (Exodus 28:3-4). The tent, or temple, consisted of the Most Holy Place and the Holy Place. The Most Holy Place represented the very presence of God. The Ark of the Covenant, containing the Ten Commandments, was placed in the Most Holy Place. The Book of the Law was placed beside the ark as a witness against the people for the sins they had committed (Deuteronomy 31:26). A thick curtain separated the Most Holy Place from the Holy Place (Exodus 26:33-34). The only one who could go through the curtain into the Most Holy Place was the High Priest, and he could enter the Most Holy Place only once a year (Exodus 30:10; Leviticus 16:34; Hebrews 9:7).

The Day Of Atonement

Every day of the year, except the Sabbath, animals were sacrificed for the known sins of the people. Once a year an animal was sacrificed for the sins the people committed in ignorance, meaning sins they were unaware they had committed. All these sacrifices temporarily covered the payment for their sins, but they never permanently took away the payment.

The once a year sacrifice was called the Day of Atonement (Leviticus 16:31). On the Day of Atonement, the High Priest would take the blood of the animal sacrificed and sprinkle it on the cover of the Ark of the Covenant (Leviticus 16:15). This cover was known as the mercy seat and signified God's mercy toward the people of Israel for their sins. On this day, the payment for the unknown sins would be temporarily covered, cleansing them temporarily from all the unknown sins of the previous year (Leviticus 16:30). For a day, they would rest in this covering and cleansing (Leviticus 16:31). Yet, the next day their sins would be counted against them until the next sacrifice.

Resting from their sins was never permanent, only temporal. Following the Day of Atonement, other animal sacrifices for sins started. These sacrifices were made day after day after day. As a result, the work of the High Priest and the other priests was never done. Day after day and year after year, they continually sacrificed animals to temporarily cover the payment for their own sins and the sins of the people (Hebrews 5:3; 7:27; 10:11). They did this for fifteen-hundred years.

A Temporary Washing

The old covenant was much like washing clothes. Clothes are always getting dirty, needing to be cleaned. So we wash clothes day after day after day and year after year after year. They are clean one day and dirty the next. Then one Saturday, we have the Day of Washing. We wash all our clothes. They are clean. That's good news. We can rest. Let's celebrate. All our clothes are clean! But only temporarily. The next day, the dirty clothes start piling up again. And we start washing clothes again. Thus, the cycle continues...day after day after day, year after year after year...for the rest of our lives.

The Book Of Grace

Day after day after day, and year after year after year, the old covenant was like a washing machine, temporarily cleansing people from their sins. However, these sacrifices were only a shadow of the real sacrifice to come, the sacrifice of Jesus (Colossians 2:17; Hebrews 10:1). With the sacrifice of Jesus for all sins, for all people, for all time, the permanent forgiveness and cleansing of sins came. Through the death of Jesus, the old covenant came to an end and the new covenant was ushered in (Hebrews 7:18-19). The Book of the Covenant was closed, and the *"Book of Grace"* or new covenant of grace was opened.

Holding On To The Old Covenant

The new covenant of grace is found in detail in the Bible, especially Hebrews. Hebrews was written to Jewish people to convince them Jesus ushered in the new covenant of grace, bringing an end to the old covenant of law. However, many of them wanted to hold on to the old covenant of law, even though the new covenant of grace had replaced it (Hebrews 8:7-8; 10:9).

Holding on to the old covenant, after it had been replaced by the new covenant, would be like a family continuing to hold on to a picture of a loved one who was away from home for a long time, even though their loved one returned home and was standing in front of them. Let me explain.

Let's say a loved one has been away from home for a very long time. Every day the family looks at the picture of the loved one who is away, longing for the day when their loved one returns. Their loved one has talked with the family, telling them he will be coming home, but he isn't sure when. They eagerly anticipate his coming, hoping each day might be the day he comes home. So every day they look at their loved one's picture, wondering if this may be the day. Then, after a long time of waiting, their loved one comes home. He is so full of joy to be home. However, rather than embracing their loved one and enjoying his return home, the family continues to hold on to and look at the picture, never acknowledging their loved one's return. No hug. No embrace. They totally ignore him, as if he never came home, and continue to hold on to his picture, longing for his return.

This describes the very purpose for which Hebrews was written. The continual sacrifices in the old covenant were only pictures of the coming of Jesus and his final sacrifice for sins. He is the one the pictures of the old covenant represented and the one for whom the people of Israel were longing. But when he came, many continued to look at the pictures, totally ignoring and completely rejecting the coming of Jesus. As a result, they continued to hold on to and look at the sacrificial pictures day after day after day with each animal sacrifice, when the real sacrifice, Jesus, was crucified right before their very eyes.

Leave The Elementary School Of The Old Covenant

The anticipation of the coming of the Christ to be the final sacrifice for sins was considered an elementary teaching by the writer of Hebrews (Hebrews 6:1-3). He compared the old covenant of law to elementary school, or the ABC's and 123's of the coming of the Christ. Now that Jesus had come and brought righteousness by faith, they should graduate from the elementary school of law and go on to maturity in the graduate school of grace. As a matter of fact, the writer tells them they should be teaching the new covenant of grace rather than re-learning again and again the elementary teachings of the Book of the Covenant and the prophecies of the coming of the Christ. Now that Christ had come, died, and was resurrected from the dead, they needed to move on by studying and teaching the *"Book of Grace"*, or the new covenant (Hebrews 5:11-14).

Paul, in 2 Corinthians 3:6, wrote that God had made him a competent minister or teacher of the new covenant. In the same way, the author of Hebrews is encouraging the people to become competent teachers of the new covenant of grace.

The Old Covenant Is A Conditional Covenant Of Blessings And Curses

The old covenant at one time governed the relationship between God and Israel. It was a conditional covenant requiring obedience to the Ten Commandments and prescribing the sacrifices for sins for not obeying them. It was a covenant of condemnation (2 Corinthians 3:6-9). This is why it was placed beside the Ark of the Covenant in the Most Holy Place as a witness against the sins of the people, testifying they were deserving of condemnation, yet an innocent animal was condemned in their place.

The old covenant, being a conditional covenant, was an *if-then* covenant. If they obeyed God, he would bless them. If they disobeyed curses would come upon them (Deuteronomy 28). The desire of God was for them to be blessed not cursed. He wanted to protect them from destruction and make them the most beautiful and blessed nation on earth (Jeremiah 3:19). From Israel, all the other nations and people of the world would be blessed abundantly!

The Promise Of A New Covenant of Grace

However, they did not follow the Book of the Covenant. They did not fulfill the "if" part of the covenant. They turned away from God and worshipped the false gods of surrounding nations. The curses came upon them (Jeremiah 11:6-8), but God told them a new covenant would come (Jeremiah 31:33-34; Hebrews 8:8-13).

The new covenant is an eternal covenant of grace (Hebrews 13:20) based upon the blood of Jesus (Hebrews 2:9). It replaced the old covenant of law (Hebrews 8:7; 9:10; 10:9). The new covenant is for all people. It brings complete forgiveness (Hebrews 8:12; 10:17-18) and reconciles people to God in a love relationship. Our relationship with God is based upon the new covenant of grace, meaning all that God has done for us in Jesus.

God Writes His Love On Our Hearts

With the new covenant in full operation, God, through the Spirit of Jesus, writes his love on the minds and hearts of those responding to his grace (Hebrews 8:10). Everyone participating in the new covenant, through faith in Jesus, knows God and is known by him (Hebrews 10:11).

The ultimate fulfillment of the new covenant will happen when God creates the new earth. On the new earth, God will live among us (Jeremiah 24:7; 32:38-41; Ezekiel 27:24-28; Revelation 21:1-4). He will dwell in love among his people, bringing peace, joy, healing, forgiveness, and righteousness to all people everywhere. Anyone desiring to be a part of his kingdom is invited. Anyone who has been left parched by the world's false promises, anyone who is feeling the shame, guilt, and condemnation of their sins is invited to come and drink from the spring of the water of life...Jesus (Revelation 21:1-6).

God Forgives Our Sins

The new covenant of grace is a covenant God fulfills on behalf of mankind. Through the new covenant of grace, Jesus died for the sins of everyone (Hebrews 2:9). As a result, God forgave our sins and remembers them no more (Jeremiah 31:34; Hebrews 8:12; 10:17-18).

By remembering our sins no more, God no longer keeps a record of our sins.

Why does God no longer remember or keep a record of our sins? The reason is because all our sins were counted against Jesus. There is no record. It was nailed to the cross with Jesus. There are no sins for God to remember.

Many people live in fear, falsely believing God remembers their sins and counts their sins against them. But the good news of the new covenant of grace is that God remembers our sins no more because they were counted against Jesus (2 Corinthians 5:18-19).

God Puts His Spirit In Our Hearts

Because the new covenant of grace results in the forgiveness of our sins, God sends the Spirit of Jesus into our hearts (Ezekiel 36:25-28; Galatians 4:6). Through his Spirit, he pours his love into our hearts (Deuteronomy 30:6; Romans 5:5). We now call him "Abba, Father" (Romans 8:14-16; Galatians 4:6).

We Experience The New Covenant By Faith

For those who respond with faith to his grace freely given to us through Jesus, we begin to experience and enjoy the new covenant in our hearts. We experience and enjoy God's forgiveness of all our sins. We experience and enjoy the presence of his Spirit in our hearts, enabling us to call God our loving Father. We experience and enjoy the growth and change grace produces within us.

Jesus: Fully God, Fully Man

We saw at the beginning of this chapter that Jesus ushered in the new covenant when he died. Hebrews 9:15 tells us that Jesus was the mediator of the new covenant [testament]. A mediator stands between two people, fully representing both. Jesus fully represented God in a human body. He also fully represented mankind by becoming human. Hebrews chapter one tells us Jesus is one hundred percent God. Hebrews chapter two tells us Jesus is one hundred percent man.

In the Bible, Jesus is called both the Son of God (Luke 22:70), meaning fully God, and the Son of Man (Luke 19:10), meaning fully man. The phrase *Son of* in the Bible means "having the very nature of". James and John were called Sons of Thunder (Mark 3:17). This means they had thunderous natures. Barnabas was called Son of Encouragement (Acts 4:36). This means he had an encouraging nature. In being called Son of God and Son of Man, Jesus had the complete nature of God and the complete nature of man, with the exception that his human nature was without sin (Hebrews 4:15).

Being fully God and fully man, Jesus was the mediator between God and mankind. He fully represented God's justice and love in paying our sin penalty through his death. He fully represented mankind in paying for our sins in his body, providing forgiveness of our sins through his blood. Therefore, Jesus became the guarantor of God's eternal covenant of grace (Hebrews 7:22; Hebrews 13:20).

This act of Jesus paying the penalty for our sins is God's story of grace to bring us into a relationship himself. Hebrews 2:9 says, "*...so that by the grace of God he* [Jesus] *might taste death for everyone.*" It was by God's grace given freely to us through the death of Jesus that the new covenant of grace was brought to the human race, making it possible for us to be reconciled to God in a love relationship. The new covenant reveals God's heart of love for the human race and his desire to be in a relationship with each of us.

Reconciliation, or being in a love relationship with us, is the desire of God's heart. He longs to be in a love relationship with each of us. That is why in the new covenant *"God was reconciling the world to himself in Christ, not counting people's sins against them"* (2 Corinthians 5:19). In the old covenant of law, sin kept people out of a love relationship with God. But now, by grace, Jesus has taken all our sins upon himself, completely removing them, so they no longer prevent us from being in a relationship with God.

God now gives us the choice to be reconciled to him (2 Corinthians 5:20). We receive this reconciliation by faith in Jesus (Romans 5:11). For those who receive reconciliation, the old covenant of law is gone, and the new covenant of grace has come (2 Corinthians 5:17)!

The New Covenant Is A Better Covenant

The New Covenant Draws Us Close To God

The book of Hebrews describes the new covenant of grace as a better covenant than the old covenant of law (Hebrews 7:19, 22). It is better because grace draws us close to God in an authentic relationship where we can be transparent and honest with him, assured of his love, kindness, and forgiveness. Because of grace, we come into the presence of God, the throne of grace (Hebrews 4:16), without guilt or condemnation, fully assured God keeps no record of our sins, since our sins have been forgiven forever through the death of Jesus.

The law could not draw us close to God. The law convicted us of sin and brought death (Romans 7:14-25; 2 Corinthians 3:6-7). The law could not bring eternal forgiveness. The law could not eternally remove our guilt and shame. The law remembered our sins by keeping a record of them. The law only covered the payment for our sins temporarily but never removed them eternally. Consequently, people living under the old covenant of law lived in constant condemnation, guilt, and shame, afraid to go into the presence of God.

The New Covenant Eternally And Completely Pays Our Sin Penalty

The old covenant of law was like going out to eat with a friend, then, after eating the meal, realizing you had no money to pay for your meal. So, you ask your friend to cover the amount of your meal until you can pay him back. He pays for your meal, but you still need to pay him back. He didn't remove the payment for your meal, he covered it. Now, rather than owing the restaurant money, you owe your friend money. The payment you owe was simply transferred from the restaurant to your friend. You still owe a debt.

This is a description of the old covenant. We have a payment for our sins called death. Rather than making the payment, an innocent animal covered the payment for the sins of people under the old covenant when the payment was transferred to the animal. The animal was then sacrificed, covering the death penalty for the sins of those living under the law. The animal did not remove the sin debt; it only covered it until Jesus came. The payment still needed to be made.

Now imagine you are eating a meal in a restaurant with another friend. Once again, you do not have any money to pay for your meal. You ask your friend to cover your meal until you can pay him back. However, the friend responds by saying he will completely pay for your meal, telling you not to worry about paying him back. The meal was free to you because it was purchased by someone else. By faith, you receive the free meal provided for you by your friend, telling him *"Thank you."*

That is what Jesus did for us. He did not cover the payment for our sins temporarily until we could pay him back. Instead, he completely paid our sin penalty, laying down his life for his friends (John 15:13).

John, when seeing Jesus, said, *"Look, the Lamb of God, who takes away the sin of the world!"* (John 1:29). 1 John 2:2 says Jesus took away the penalty for the sins of the whole world by paying it for us through his death. This is the story of grace! And we simply say, *"Thank you"*, living the rest of our lives in gratitude for his grace (2 Corinthians 4:15).

Through the new covenant, Jesus died for all people, for all sin, for all time when he sacrificed himself for our sins (Hebrews 7:27; 9:26; 10:10, 12). Through his blood, he eternally and completely paid for the sins of all people (Hebrews 9:12). He then took his shed blood into the very presence of God, heaven itself, as the full, final, and forever payment for our sins (Hebrews 9:12, 26).

"Here Is My Blood, I Paid It All"

Understanding this part of the story of grace impacted my life greatly. The fact that Jesus would willingly offer himself as a sacrifice for the full, final, and forever payment for my sins and then carry his blood into the very presence of God for my forgiveness transformed my life. I could picture Jesus saying to his Father, *"Father, here is my blood poured out for Brad for the forgiveness of his sins. I have paid his sin penalty in full and forever. It is final. It is finished. Brad has no debt to pay. I paid it all."* He not only paid for my sins, he paid for yours, too. He loves you! He has forgiven you!

"I Will Forgive And Remember Their Sins No More"

Because of the sacrifice of Jesus for our sins, God remembers our sins no more. He keeps no record of our sins. Our sins have been forgiven. The Bible says, *"For I will forgive their wickedness and remember their sins no more*" (Hebrews 8:12) and "*Their sins and lawless acts I will remember no more*" (Hebrews 10:17).

"*Thank You!*"

Since our sins have been completely paid for by Jesus, there is no need for any more sacrifices for sins (Hebrews 8:12; 10:17-18). Jesus himself said, "*It is finished*" (John 19:30). According the very words of Jesus, he has made the full, final, and forever payment for our sins. There is no need to worry anymore if your sins are forgiven. You simply receive his forgiveness by faith and tell him "*Thank you*" (2 Corinthians 4:15; Colossians 2:6-7; Hebrews 13:15), praising him for the grace he has freely given you in providing for the forgiveness of all your sins (Ephesians 1:6-8).

When I began thanking and praising God for the forgiveness he fully, freely, and forever gave me by grace through Jesus, my life changed. When I began thanking and praising him for the forgiveness he had given me in Jesus, rather than continuing to ask him for what he had already provided, my life changed. When I stopped asking him to give me more forgiveness but rather accepted by faith the forgiveness he already fully provided for me in the new covenant, my life changed. When I stopped confessing all my sins to God, so I could be forgiven, but rather claimed he had already forgiven all my sins by grace through Jesus, my life changed. I knew the story of God's grace had intersected with the story of my life when I began to thank him and praise him for forgiveness rather than trying to get what he had already freely given.

Hard Hearts To The New Covenant

Even though Jesus completely paid the sin penalty for all people, for all sins, for all time, many of those living under the old covenant of law, the Book of the Covenant, ignored (Hebrews 2:3) or completely rejected his payment and continued to sacrifice animals for the forgiveness of sins. With each animal sacrifice in the temple, they were falling away from grace by crucifying Jesus all over again (Hebrews 6:6) and trampling under foot his blood (Hebrews 10:29), insulting the Spirit of grace (Hebrews 10:29). They refused to receive God's grace freely provided for them through Jesus. Their hearts were hardened in unbelief to the grace provided for them in Jesus (3:12-13).

Refusing To Enter The Promised Land Of Grace

The author of Hebrews writes about the hardening of their hearts to grace by comparing their generation with the generation that refused to enter the Promised Land after Moses had delivered the people from Egyptian slavery. Just like the people hardened their hearts, refusing to enter the Promised Land in Canaan, the land flowing with milk and honey, the people hardened their hearts to the new covenant of grace and refused to enter the Promised Land of Grace, the land flowing with love, forgiveness, righteousness, peace, joy, and life (Hebrews 3:7-4:11). Even though God had delivered them from slavery to the Book of the Covenant, they chose instead to wander in the desert of their own shame, guilt, and condemnation by rejecting his grace.

The writer of Hebrews encouraged his non-believing, Jewish brothers to not have a disobedient, sinful, unbelieving heart like their forefathers did when they refused to enter the Promised Land. He encouraged them not to reject the Promised Land of the new covenant of grace by continuing to rely on the old covenant of law for forgiveness, righteousness, and acceptance with God (Hebrews 3:12, 19; 4:6, 11). If they rejected grace, they would wander in the wilderness of law, or the wilderness of shame, guilt, and condemnation for the rest of their lives, eventually dying in the desert of spiritual dryness and misery (Hebrews 3:16-19). However, if they accepted grace through faith, they could enter the Promised Land of Grace, resting forever in God's love, forgiveness, and righteousness (Hebrews 4:2-3).

Resting In Grace Is Available For All

The writer of the book of Hebrews tells us the promise of resting in God's grace is available for all. His desire is for no one to fall short of entering the Promised Land of Grace. The only reason some people some come short of entering grace is unbelief, or not combining what they hear about grace with faith. Instead of combining what they hear about grace with faith, they continue to act disobediently to God by hardening their hearts to grace and by depending upon their own religious works and morality to gain God's forgiveness, acceptance, and righteousness.

Falling Away From Grace

This is exactly what many of those who heard about the good news of the new covenant of grace were doing in the book of Hebrews. Initially, they experienced the miracles of Jesus as the Christ, confirming he was the Christ. Through these miracles, they had tasted of the age to come, the coming kingdom on the new earth (Hebrews 2:3-4; 6:4-6). But when Jesus was crucified, they turned back to the dead works of Book of the Covenant, such as sacrificing animals in the temple, as the means for obtaining God's forgiveness and righteousness, which was an impossibility now that grace had come (Hebrews 6:4-6; Hebrews 10:4).

By doing this, they fell away from the new covenant of grace and were now crucifying Jesus all over again with each animal they sacrificed, devaluing the blood of Jesus for all to see (Hebrews 6:6). With each sacrificed animal, they were trampling underfoot the precious blood of Jesus (Hebrews 10:29). They were valuing the blood of sacrificed animals over the blood of Jesus, and, in doing so, were making a mockery of his blood by treating it with such disgrace (Hebrews 6:6). They were deliberately committing the sin of unbelief through a hard heart toward grace. By rejecting grace, all they could look forward to was the fearful expectation of God's judgment to come (Hebrews 10:26).

Jesus Sat Down

Since many rejected the new covenant of grace, including many of the priests, the priests continued the daily and yearly sacrifices of animals for the sins of the people (Hebrews 10:11). The work of the priests under the old covenant was never finished. They stood day after day and year after year sacrificing animals to cover their own sins and the sins of the people. They could never rest (Hebrews 10:11). There was always another animal to be sacrificed to cover their own sins and the sins of others (Hebrews 5:1-3). But Jesus was the final High Priest. He was the final sacrifice. When Jesus offered himself as the final sacrifice for all sin, for all people, for all time, he sat down at the right hand of God (Hebrews 1:3; 10:12).

Seated With Christ

This act of Jesus sitting down is symbolic of his payment for the sins of all people being complete and eternal...finished forever. Jesus now rested from his work of paying our sin penalty through his shed blood. The Bible says we have been seated with Christ in the heavenly realms (Ephesians 2:6). Those who have received God's grace through faith in Jesus can rest, too!

We can rest from trying to make sure all our sins are confessed to stay in fellowship with God. We no longer must seek to maintain God's forgiveness through religious works or endless confession. We do not have to try to maintain fellowship with God by keeping short accounts on sin. This account doesn't even exist! It has been paid in full by Jesus.

We can rest from having to meet the requirements of spiritual disciplines, worrying that we have not prayed or read our Bible enough, or missed a quiet time. We can rest from the misery of wandering in the wilderness of shame, guilt, and condemnation. We rest from this wilderness by entering God's Promised Land of Grace, where we enjoy a land flowing with love, forgiveness, peace, righteousness, and acceptance. A land where he remembers our sins no more!

Enjoying A Relationship With God

The Promised Land of the new covenant of grace is much more than just experiencing God's complete forgiveness, as wonderful as his forgiveness is. The Promised Land of grace also includes enjoying a relationship with God. It is a covenant based upon a love relationship with God where we know him in intimate, authentic way, and he knows us (Hebrews 8:10-11). He writes his laws of love in our minds and on our hearts (Hebrews 8:10), a love for God and a love for others based on his love for us. This love relationship with God changes our hearts and lives.

We Go Confidently Into God's Presence

In this relationship with God, we go confidently into the very presence of God, the very presence of grace itself (Ephesians 2:18; 3:12; Hebrews 4:16). We do not have to earn our way into his presence through religious activities and morality, as if we ever could. Rather, we come as we are into his presence, assured of his love, acceptance, and kindness. We talk freely with him about what is on our hearts and what is happening in our lives. We no longer must hide our sins from him, trying to cover them with religious works, trying to eliminate them through our endless confession, or trying to run from him out of fear. Instead, we talk freely and openly with God about our joys, hopes, dreams, desires, doubts, fears, problems, troubles, concerns, struggles, weaknesses, and sins.

We Can Be Open And Honest With God

The great fear of many Bible teachers is people will use grace as a license to sin, even though the Bible clearly states it is grace that removes us from the power and control of sin (Romans 6:14; Titus 2:11-14). They fear people will develop a careless attitude and become apathetic toward sin, ultimately losing respect for God, since they no longer have "the fear of the Lord in them".

In reality, grace leads to more confession of sin because it allows us to be open and honest with God in an atmosphere of love and acceptance. This confession is not for the purpose of asking for forgiveness from God or staying in fellowship with him, but it is for the purpose of having a real relationship with God. A relationship that includes openness and honesty about our sins without fear of rejection or condemnation.

True confession is being honest with God. Only grace can produce honesty with God because grace removes all fear of condemnation and judgment from him (1 John 4:16-18). We can never be honest and open if we are afraid of someone. Actually, we will try to get away from this person, running and hiding if necessary.

No More Running And Hiding From God

Running and hiding from God are what many people do. The story of his grace has never intersected with the story of their lives. So, they keep running and hiding, never realizing God desires an open, honest relationship with them.

Running and hiding from God is what Charles did in his addiction. Charles and I spent hours discussing grace. I had given him many resources on grace, including Bob George's book *"Why Jesus Changes Everything."* After reading these resources and Bob's book, he told me that what kept him in his cycle of addiction was running and hiding from God because he did not understand God's grace.

He was trying to numb the feelings of condemnation, guilt, and shame arising from his addiction. He did not understand he could come to God openly and honestly with the sinful desires he was having. He did not understand he was completely forgiven by God and in continual fellowship with God where he could talk openly with God assured of his love and acceptance.

He felt God was looking down upon him in anger, judgment, and condemnation. He believed he could never experience closeness with God again. However, as he began to understand grace, he began to be set free from the condemnation, guilt, and shame that sin brings. He began to understand he was completely forgiven, loved, and accepted by God and in fellowship with him. As a result, he could now have an open and honest relationship with God. The story of God's grace had intersected with the story of his life, changing it forever.

Another person who ran and hid from God for years was Karen. Like Charles, Karen was living in deep guilt and shame because of sin. She felt she could never have a close relationship with God again. There was a time in her life when she was close to God. But years of sin took her away from the close, intimate relationship with God she once enjoyed. She was convinced her relationship with God was beyond recovery. My wife and I spent hours with her, sharing with her about grace. As grace began penetrating her heart, she began to be healed. The intimate relationship she once had with God was soon restored by grace.

Today, Karen is not only enjoying a close relationship with God, but she is also enjoying a relationship with her family. Grace not only brought about recovery in her relationship with God, but it also restored relationships with her family as well.

We Talk Freely With God

The old covenant of law, including the Ten Commandments, could never produce an open, honest relationship with God. All it could produce was condemnation and death (2 Corinthians 3:7, 9). But now in Christ, the old covenant of condemnation and death has been removed. The condemnation of the Ten Commandments has been removed (2 Corinthians 3:14). Jesus lives in us, freeing us from the bondage of the law and patiently transforming our lives through his Spirit (2 Corinthians 3:16-18).

We no longer relate to God under the old covenant of law but under the new covenant of grace. The old covenant of law is gone, and the new covenant of grace has come (2 Corinthians 5:17). Through the new covenant of grace, we talk freely with God, not only about our sins, but also about our problems, pain, and sufferings.

Jesus Can Sympathize With Us In Our Sufferings

As we talk freely with Jesus about our sufferings, he sympathizes with us. He can sympathize with us because he himself experienced tremendous hurt and heartache during his life on earth

(Isaiah 52:14-53:12; Hebrews 2:10; 5:7-9). He knows what it is like to be one of us. He was not the most handsome of all men, as portrayed in movies and paintings. There was nothing in his physical features that would cause someone to take a second look at him. If anything, people would stare at him as if he was some type of odd person. He was rejected, beaten, hit, whipped, mocked, abandoned, betrayed, misunderstood, misjudged, tortured, and abused. He was abused religiously, mentally, physically, emotionally, and in a way...sexually.

Let me explain. Whenever we see paintings of Jesus crucified on the cross, he is clothed from the waist down. Yet when Roman soldiers crucified people, they never clothed those being crucified. They weren't that kind. Those being crucified were stripped naked, as was Jesus, and paraded around for all to see, then nailed completely unclothed on the cross in full public view.

Jesus knows how it feels to be stripped down unwillingly, paraded around for all to see, and then violently exposed. So when the Bible says he can sympathize with us in our weakness, he really can. He knows what it is like to be you. He can sympathize with you in your sufferings.

"I Know How You Feel, I Love You, I Am With You"

But why did Jesus do this? Why did God, as Jesus, willingly submit himself to the sufferings of this world? Because he loves you. For God to be in an authentic relationship with you, he wanted and needed to know what it is like to be you. He wanted and needed to know what it really feels like when you come to him in your sufferings. He did not want to be a distant God, a stranger to your pain. Rather, he wanted to be the God who puts his arms around you saying, *"I know how you feel. I love you. I am with you."*

This is the story of the new covenant. It is the story of how much God loves you and wants to be in a relationship with you. It is a story of how he wants to spend eternity with you. It is the story of how he wants to set you free from shame, guilt, and condemnation as you experience his love, acceptance, kindness, forgiveness, and righteousness. It is the story of Jesus' shed blood poured out for all of your sins and where God has forgiven all of your sins, no longer counting your sins against you or recording them at all. It is story of how much he feels your hurt and pain so he can sympathize with you. It is the story of how much he longs to be with you forever in his eternal kingdom where there are no more tears, pain, hurt, heartache, mourning, or death, but only love, peace, joy, healing, and righteousness. It is the story of grace. What a marvelous story!

12

Your Story of Grace

God's heart is for the story of his grace to intersect with the story of your life, and when it does, your life will never be the same. So, what's your story?

Maybe, like me, you've lived unaware of God's grace, though you were very familiar with the word grace and thought you understood it. You could define grace as *God's unmerited favor*, sing the song *Amazing Grace*, knew the acronym G.R.A.C.E - *God's Riches At Christ's Expense*, and could quote popular verses about grace. But you are now seeing there is more to grace than you ever saw before.

When I first saw grace, flying on the airplane from Denver to Mobile while reading *Classic Christianity,* it was like putting on a new pair of glasses and seeing with sharpness objects I once saw dimly or never saw at all. Suddenly, verses in the Bible became clearer. I saw truths in the Bible I had never seen. It was exciting!

Maybe this is what is happening for you now. In reading this book, you're seeing truths about God and the Bible you never knew could be seen. Verses once a blur to you are now clearly seen.

Maybe you live under law, trying to maintain or obtain acceptance with God through religious activity, faithfulness, or morality. But you now realize your acceptance with God does not come through religious activities, faithfulness, or morality but by grace alone through faith alone.

Maybe you have set aside grace as the only way to become righteous before God and have been depending upon law. But you now realize if righteousness could be gained through the law, then Jesus died for nothing.

Maybe you live with a sense of God's rejection, believing you must achieve acceptance with God through the requirements of your religious system, denomination, or organization. But you never feel you can measure up, even though you try to be committed and faithful. However, because of grace, you realize acceptance with God is not achieved by faithfully following the requirements of a religious system, denomination, or organization but by faith in Jesus.

Maybe you feel you must read your Bible and pray every day. When you do, you feel good, but when you don't, you feel guilty. But now, because of grace, you do not see reading your Bible and prayer as requirements to be checked off the "to-do" list so you do not feel guilty all day.

Maybe you feel God is keeping a record of your sins and will one day count all your sins against you. But now, because of grace, you know God is not keeping a record of your sins and will never count your sins against you. You now understand the record of your sins was fully and permanently nailed to the cross with Jesus.

Maybe you live trying to stay in fellowship with God by making sure you have no unconfessed sin in your life. Your days are spent focusing on your sin, wondering and worrying if you have confessed them all but are never sure. This leaves you wondering if you are in fellowship with God. Now, because of grace, you can focus on Jesus who loved you and gave his life for you, assured he is the one who guarantees your fellowship with God.

Maybe you spend your days in bondage daily asking God to forgive you. Because of grace, you now live in the freedom of God's forgiveness, thanking him you are fully forgiven forever!

Maybe you live trying to keep short accounts on sin because you were told that if you die with unconfessed sin, you will lose your salvation and go to hell. As a result, your days are spent in mental torment because you fear you may have missed a sin or that you may die suddenly and not have the opportunity to confess your sins. Because of grace, you no longer have to live in fear. You now enjoy your relationship with God.

Maybe you were told you could lose your salvation and believe you have. You are now living your life in discouragement and depression. Because of grace, your salvation is eternal. You will always be God's child. To lose your salvation means your relationship with God could be severed. Because of grace, your salvation is eternally secure. Nothing will ever separate you from your relationship with God...nothing!

Maybe you feel God could never forgive you for certain sins, so you keep him at a distance or out of your life altogether. But you now know your sins are forgiven and you can draw close to God.

Maybe you feel like you have let God down and he will not have you back. But the truth is you can't disappoint God. He has never left you. He permanently dwells within your heart through the Spirit of Jesus.

Maybe, because of shame and guilt, you feel like you can never be close to God again. You keep him at a distance. But through grace, God is drawing you close to himself.

Maybe you made promises to God that you have broken and feel you must earn your way back into his heart. The truth is you never had to make promises to God, and you have always been in his heart.

Maybe you thought you fell from grace because of sin in your life. But now you realize you have fallen into grace.

Maybe you have been held captive by the words of others. You no longer have to be held captive by their words. By faith, you can be set free by God's word of grace.

Maybe you have been relating to God as a judge, living in condemnation and fearing his judgment. Because of grace, you can now relate to God as your Father, enjoying his love and forgiveness as his child.

Maybe you feel like the tragic events of your life were God's punishment for your sins. But now you realize Jesus paid the penalty for all your sins and God is not punishing you.

Maybe you have been punishing yourself for sins in your life. You no longer have to punish yourself, because Jesus paid your sin penalty in full.

Maybe you have been living in fear of where you will spend eternity. But you have come to understand eternal life is through belief in Jesus alone. You can live in peace now.

Maybe you feel like God has forgiven you, but you have not been able forgive yourself. Now, through grace, you are able to forgive yourself.

Maybe you are having trouble forgiving someone but fear if you don't, God will not forgive you. But now that you understand the new covenant of grace, you realize all your sins are forgiven, and in time, you will find it possible to do what was at one time impossible, forgive the person who hurt you.

Maybe you feel so guilty about your past that you can't imagine a life without guilt. But now your guilt is being replaced by God's grace.

Maybe you have been running and hiding from God, fearing his judgment and condemnation. But because of grace, you know you can come to him in an open and honest relationship, assured of his love, acceptance, and forgiveness.

Maybe you live with an addiction, trying to numb the pain of your guilt, shame, or suffering. But because of grace, you no longer have to numb your pain. You can bring it to God.

Maybe you suffer daily because you have been beaten, mocked, abandoned, betrayed, misunderstood, misjudged, tortured, or abused. You were abused religiously, mentally, physically, emotionally, or sexually. But now you know Jesus understands how you feel and sympathizes with you. In him, you find grace and mercy to strengthen you in your suffering.

Maybe you have been living as a modern-day Pharisee, proud of your religious activity and morality, while demanding others repent of their sins, not realizing you are no different and need to repent of the sin of self-righteousness.

Maybe you are a Bible teacher or Pastor and realize you have been teaching the Bible inaccurately. But now you are seeing the story of God's grace in the Bible and desire to teach the story of grace to your church regardless of the response of the leaders and members within your church.

Maybe you are a mom or dad who has been raising your children by law rather than grace. But you now desire to raise your children in God's unconditional love, unearned blessings, unmerited kindness, and unlimited forgiveness.

Maybe you are a husband or wife who has been relating to your spouse by law not grace. By realizing you do not live under the judgment and condemnation of the law, you are no longer going to subject your spouse to your law. Because Jesus has served you in love, you now desire to serve your spouse in love.

Maybe you have been controlled by anger in your relationships. But through the Father's love for you, you are now being controlled by his love, peace, patience, kindness, goodness, and gentleness.

Maybe you have made people the object of your anger. Now you desire to make them the object of grace, freely giving them the grace that God has given you.

Maybe you have been filled with bitterness. But through grace, God is filling you with his love and forgiveness.

Maybe all of us have come to see our imperfections because of our sins. But in our sinful imperfections, the story of God's grace has intersected with the story of our lives, and we now realize we fall into his grace...his unconditional love, unearned blessings, unmerited kindness, and unlimited forgiveness freely given to us through Jesus.

Maybe through this book, the story of God's grace has intersected with the story of your life, and your life will never be the same!

Maybe you are broken...poor in spirit...mourning your sinful condition, hungering and thirsting for God's love, forgiveness, and acceptance. You now know God's grace is available to you.

Maybe you are telling yourself you do not deserve to place your faith in Jesus. You have done too much, gone too far, or ignored God too long, but that is what grace is all about. God's grace is unending and undeserving. His grace gives us what we don't deserve.

Will you accept God's free offer of grace to you by placing your faith in Jesus? He loves you!

If you would like to place your faith in Jesus, here is a simple prayer to do so.

God, I realize I was created to be in a love relationship with you. I admit I have sinned and am not in a relationship with you. But through grace, you have made it possible for me to be in a love relationship with you. Because of your great love and kindness, Jesus came to earth to pay my sin penalty through his blood. Jesus died for all of my sins. Because all my sins were counted against Jesus in his death, you are no longer counting my sins against me. I accept your forgiveness by faith. I believe Jesus arose from the dead and ascended into heaven and will one day return to establish his eternal kingdom of love, peace, joy, healing, and righteousness on earth. God, I want to begin a relationship with you and live in your eternal kingdom. Today, I place my faith in Jesus. I am fully forgiven and accepted by you, in a love relationship with you, and will one day live forever in your kingdom.

If you placed your faith in Jesus, I celebrate with you! All of heaven celebrates with you!

A Note Of Encouragement

In Galatians 5:1, Paul encouraged the Galatians to stand firm in their freedom of grace by telling them, "*It is for freedom that Christ has set us free. Stand firm, then, and do not let yourselves be burdened again by a yoke of slavery.*" Paul knew the religious leaders surrounding Galatia did not embrace grace and they would seek to enslave, once again, the Galatian people by persuading them to seek God's righteousness through adhering to the religious and moral standard of the Law of Moses, which he called a "yoke of bondage".

He exhorted them, since it was Christ who set them free, to stand firm in their freedom when these religious leaders tried to push them away from grace and back to the law for acceptance with God. Maintaining their freedom by standing firm in grace was the right action for them to take because Christ was the one who set them free from the law through his death and resurrection.

Just as Paul encouraged and exhorted the Galatian grace believers to stand firm in their freedom, I want to do the same with you. Christ has set you free from seeking to gain God's righteousness by adhering to any religious or moral standard. You no longer need to seek God's acceptance, forgiveness, or fellowship by following any organization's, ministry's, church's, pastor's, or leader's requirements or teachings.

Many non-grace-based leaders, churches, and ministries will attempt to burden you again with their requirements for obtaining or maintaining God's acceptance, forgiveness, or fellowship. They will tell you to pray more, read your Bible more, serve more, participate more, confess more, attend more, worship more, do more...fast, tithe, join, be all in for Jesus...and the list goes on and on. Stand firm. No person set you free. It was Christ who set you free by his grace. Therefore, since Christ set you free, stand firm in grace.

It is okay not to follow the requirements and teachings of others...they are only people...they are not Jesus. They didn't die to set you free, Jesus did. So, it is okay to not allow them to steal the freedom that grace brings. It is okay to disagree with and disconnect from them. Don't let them move you away from grace.

I have watched friends of mine who were once established in and excited about grace, drift back to a work's oriented, law-based mentality where they began to relate to God by meeting certain expectations and having certain experiences required by their church or religious organization. This was because they allowed themselves to be influenced by law-based pastors and people, those who mixed law and grace. I encourage you to permanently drop your anchor into the ocean of God's grace. Let no one pull it up.

We live in a great time. There is a growing number of believers who are understanding the good news of God's grace. They are passionate about sharing God's grace with others and supporting others on their journey of grace. They would love for you to be connected to them. They will be a wonderful source of encouragement to you.

You may also check out my website and Facebook pages, as well as my YouTube channel. There you will find resources to help you grow on your grace journey.

Thank you so much for taking the time to read my book, *The Story of Grace*. My prayer is the story of God's grace has intersected with the story of your life, and your life will never be the same!

ABOUT THE AUTHOR

In 1991, the story of God's grace intersected with the story of Brad's life when he read a book by Bob George called *Classic Christianity*. Since this time, his passion has been to share the life-changing truths of God's grace with as many people as possible in as many ways as possible. Some of the ways Brad shares the good news of God's grace is through writing, social media, and speaking.

In addition to *The Story of Grace*, Brad has written *Addicted To Grace*. This book is designed for those with addictions, yet it is recommended for anyone who struggles with sin in certain areas of their lives, or for those who want to learn more about God's grace. He has also written a booklet called *Paul and James: Were They Really In Agreement?* Both are available on his website as E-books.

Brad's website is www.simplygrace.info. You may also visit his YouTube channel and Facebook page.

For 13 years, he served as founder and Senior Pastor of Grace Church Gulf Coast. Prior to this, he attended Dallas Theological Seminary where he received a Master of Arts Degree in Christian Education. In addition, he served on staff with Campus Crusade for Christ for two years.

He holds a Bachelor of Science Degree in Coaching and Sports Administration from the University of Southern Mississippi. He is married to Becky. Together they have three sons, Kyle, Philip, and Mark.

If you would like to contact Brad about speaking at your church, conference, retreat, or event, email him at bradr1966@gmail.com.